ALL MY RELATIONS

ALL MY RELATIONS

An Anthology of Contemporary Canadian Native Fiction

Edited by Thomas King

M&S

Canadian Cataloguing in Publication Data

Main entry under title:

All my relations : an anthology of contemporary Canadian native fiction

ISBN 0-7710-6706-2

1. Canadian fiction (English) – Indian authors.*
2. Canadian fiction (English) – 20th century.

I. King, Thomas, 1943–

PS8321.A58 1990 C813'.5408'0897 C90-093330-5
PR9197.33.I53A58 1990

We acknowledge the financial support of the Government of Canada through the Book Publishing Industry Development Program for our publishing activities. We further acknowledge the support of the Canada Council for the Arts and the Ontario Arts Council for our publishing program.

Printed and bound in Canada

Design: Tania Craan

McClelland & Stewart Inc.
The Canadian Publishers
481 University Avenue
Toronto, Ontario
M5G 2E9

5 6 7 8 9 10 03 02 01 00 99 98

For Harry Robinson
(1900–1990)

CREDITS

Peter Blue Cloud's "Weaver Spider's Web" is from *Elderberry Flute Song: Contemporary Coyote Tales*, 1989, White Pine Press, Fredonia, New York. Reprinted by permission of the publisher. Joan Crate's "Welcome to the Real World" (titled for this anthology) is an excerpt from her novel, *Breathing Water*, published as part of the Nunatak Fiction Series by NeWest Publishers, Edmonton, 1989. Reprinted by permission of the publisher. The excerpt from Tomson Highway's play, *The Rez Sisters*, 1988, is reprinted by permission of Fifth House Publishers, Saskatoon. Basil H. Johnston's "Summer Holidays in Spanish" is from *Indian School Days*, published by Key Porter Books, © 1988 Key Porter Books Ltd. Reprinted by permission of the publisher. Maurice Kenny's "Rain" is from *Rain and Other Stories*, a chapbook published by Blue Cloud Quarterly Press, Marvin, South Dakota. Reprinted by permission of the author. Jovette Marchessault's "Song One: The Riverside" is from her novel, *Mother of the Grass*, translated by Yvonne M. Klein, © Jovette Marchessault and Yvonne M. Klein, Talon Books Ltd., Vancouver, 1989. Reprinted by permission of the publisher. Harry Robinson's "Captive in an English Circus" (titled in this volume "An Okanagan Indian Becomes a Captive Circus Showpiece in England"), transcribed by Wendy Wickwire, is from *Write It on Your Heart*, © Wendy Wickwire and published by Talon Books Ltd., Vancouver, 1989. Reprinted by permission of the publisher. Ruby Slipperjack's "Coal Oil, Crayons and Schoolbooks" is from her novel, *Honour the Sun*, Pemmican Publications, Inc., Winnipeg. Reprinted by permission of the publisher.

The following stories appeared in *Canadian Fiction Magazine*, No. 60, Toronto, 1987:

"An Afternoon in Bright Sunlight" by S. Bruised Head (reprinted in *The Last Map Is the Heart: Western Canadian Fiction*, Thistledown Press, Saskatoon, 1990); "Compatriots" by Emma Lee Warrior; "King of the Raft" by Daniel David Moses; "The Last Raven" by Richard G. Green; "An Okanagan Indian Becomes a Captive Circus Showpiece in England" by Harry Robinson; "Run" by Barry Milliken; "Summer Holidays in Spanish" by Basil H. Johnston.

Contents

Introduction

"All my relations" is the English equivalent of a phrase familiar to most Native peoples in North America. It may begin or end a prayer or a speech or a story, and, while each tribe has its own way of expressing this sentiment in its own language, the meaning is the same.

"All my relations" is at first a reminder of who we are and of our relationship with both our family and our relatives. It also reminds us of the extended relationship we share with all human beings. But the relationships that Native people see go further, the web of kinship extending to the animals, to the birds, to the fish, to the plants, to all the animate and inanimate forms that can be seen or imagined. More than that, "all my relations" is an encouragement for us to accept the responsibilities we have within this universal family by living our lives in a harmonious and moral manner (a common admonishment is to say of someone that they act as if they have no relations).

Within Native cultures, as within other cultures, this world of relationships is shared through language and literature. As long as the languages remained oral, the literature was available to a particular audience. But, as Native storytellers have become bilingual – telling and writing their stories in English, French, Spanish – they have created both a more pan-Native as well as a non-Native audience.

For Native audiences, the twentieth-century phenomenon of Native storytellers from different tribes sharing their stories in a common language – through the contemporary and non-traditional forms of written poetry, prose, and drama – has helped to reinforce many of the beliefs that tribes have held individually, beliefs that tribes are now discovering they share mutually. While this has not, as yet, created what might be called a pan-Native literature, the advent of written Native literature has provided Native writers with common structures, themes, and characters which can effectively express traditional and contemporary concerns about the world and the condition of living things.

It should be said at this point that when we talk about contemporary Native literature, we talk as though we already have a definition for this body of literature when, in fact, we do not. And, when we talk about Native writers, we talk as though we have a process for determining who is a Native writer and who is not, when, in fact, we don't. What we do have is a collection of literary works by individual authors who are Native by ancestry, and our hope, as writers and critics, is that if we wait long enough, the sheer bulk of this collection, when it reaches some sort of critical mass, will present us with a matrix within which a variety of patterns can be discerned.

This waiting is neither timidity nor laziness on our part. There are a great many difficulties in trying to squeeze definitions out of what we currently have. We could simply say that Native literature is literature produced by Natives. This is a competent enough definition in that it covers both contemporary written literature and oral tribal literature, and, at the same time, insists that Native literature is literature produced by Natives and not by non-Natives, recognizing that being Native is a matter of race rather than something more transitory such as nationality. One can become a Canadian and a Canadian writer, for example, without having been born in Canada, but one is either born an Indian or one is not.

This definition – on the basis of race – however, makes a rather large assumption, a type of *dicto simpliciter*. It assumes that the matter of race imparts to the Native writer a tribal understanding of the universe, access to a distinct culture, and a literary perspective that is unattainable by non-Natives. In our discussions of Native literature, we try to imagine that there is a racial denominator which full-bloods raised in cities, half-bloods raised on farms, quarter-bloods raised on reservations, Indians adopted and raised by white families, Indians who speak their tribal language, Indians who speak only English, traditionally educated Indians, university-trained Indians, Indians with little education, and the like all share. We know, of course, that there is not. We know that this is a romantic, mystical, and, in many instances, a self-serving notion that the sheer number of cultural groups in North America, the variety of Native languages, and the varied conditions of the various tribes should immediately belie.

All of which leaves us with these questions: What, for example, do we do with writers who are not Native by birth but whose experience and knowledge may make them more perceptive writers and commentators than many writers who are Native by birth? And what do we do with writers who are Native and who have few ties to a culture or tribe and who do not write about Natives or Native culture? The most vivid examples might involve whites who were adopted or raised as Indians within an Indian community. Nationalism manages this dilemma well enough because it does not insist on the accident of birth as a *sine qua non*.

Perhaps our simple definition that Native literature is literature produced by Natives will suffice for the while providing we resist the temptation of trying to define a Native, for, as Wallace Black Elk reminds us in *Black Elk: The Sacred Ways of a Lakota*, "You know straight across the board, hardly anyone really knows what is Indian. The word *Indian* in itself really doesn't mean anything. That's how come nobody knows anything about Indians."

Whatever definitions we decide on (if we ever do), the appearance of Native stories in a written form has opened up new worlds of imagination for a non-Native audience. Most Canadians have only seen Natives through the eyes of non-Native writers, and, while many of these portrayals have been sympathetic, they have also been limited in their variety of characters, themes, structures, and images.

In large part, the majority of these works are set in the nineteenth century, a period that Native writers assiduously avoid. Some of the reasons for this avoidance are obvious. The literary stereotypes and clichés for which the period is famous have been, I think, a deterrent to many of us. Feathered warriors on Pinto ponies, laconic chiefs in full regalia, dusky, raven-haired maidens, demonic shamans with eagle-claw rattles and scalping knives are all picturesque and exciting images, but they are, more properly, servants of a non-Native imagination. Rather than try to unravel the complex relationship between the nineteenth-century Indian and the white mind, or to craft a new set of images that still reflects the time but avoids the flat, static depiction of the Native and the two-dimensional quality of the culture, most of us have consciously set our literature in the present, a period that is reasonably free of literary monoliths and which allows for greater latitude in the creation of characters and situations, and, more important, allows us the opportunity to create for ourselves and our respective cultures both a present and a future. In many ways, I remain amazed at the extent of this particular division between non-Native writers and Native writers, though perhaps we will begin to write historical novels once we discover ways to make history our own.

I said that Native literature – that is, written Native literature – has opened up new worlds of imagination for a non-Native audience. It is not that we have consciously set out to do this. It is, rather, a by-product of the choices (i.e. not writing historical novels) we have made as writers and as Natives. The two major choices that we have made so far are concerned with the relationship between oral literature and written literature and with the relationship between Native people and the idea of community, and the stories in this volume, to a great extent, reflect these choices.

There is the misconception that Native oral literature is an artifact, something that vanished as an art form in the last century. Though virtually invisible outside a tribal setting, oral literature remains a strong tradition and is one of the major influences on many Native writers. Harry Robinson's story, "An Okanagan Indian Becomes a Captive Circus Showpiece in England," is a fine example of interfusional literature, literature that blends the oral and the written. In a traditional oral story, you have the stories, the gestures, the performance, the music, as well as the storyteller. In a written story, you have only the word on the page. Yet Robinson is able to make the written word become the spoken word by insisting, through his use of rhythms, patterns, syntax, and sounds, that his story be read out loud, and, in so doing, the reader becomes the storyteller.

The influence of oral literature can also be seen in Jeannette Armstrong's "This Is a Story," Peter Blue Cloud's "Weaver Spider's Web," and Thomas King's "The One About Coyote Going West," all of which take as their main character the ubiquitous trickster figure, Coyote. The trickster is an important figure for Native writers for it allows us to create a particular kind of world in which the Judeo-Christian concern with good and evil and order and disorder is replaced with the more Native concern for balance and harmony. Armstrong's story about Koyti returning to Okanagan country to find the rivers dammed and the salmon unable to return to their homes, King's story about Coyote and the Big Mistake that she creates with her thoughts, and then can't control, and Blue Cloud's story about Coyote, Grey Fox, and Weaver Spider and how Coyote got smart, are all part of a long tradition of stories that speak to the nature of the world and the relatedness of all living things.

Shirley Bruised Head, Bruce King, and J.B. Joe also make use of elements from oral literature and traditional culture. Bruised Head's "An Afternoon in Bright Sunlight" combines contemporary and traditional worlds, allowing for both realities to exist in the same space. Bruce King's "Hookto: The Evil Entity" moves further along towards what we might be tempted to call science fiction or fantasy, but is more properly simply an example of the thematic range of oral storytelling. J.B. Joe builds her story of sorrow, loss, and healing around Native and feminist spirituality, the unifying idea of the vision, and the interconnectedness of all things.

While these stories are different, each possesses a timeless quality that speaks to some of the essential relationships that exist in traditional cultures – the relationship between humans and the animals, the relationship between humans and the land, and the relationship between reality and imagination.

A most important relationship in Native cultures is the relationship which humans share with each other, a relationship that is embodied within the idea of community. Community, in a Native sense, is not simply a place or a group of people, rather it is, as novelist Louise Erdrich describes it, a place that has been "inhabited for generations," where "the landscape becomes enlivened by a sense of group and family history." That sense of group and family history, the idea of community, is the focal point for the selection from Tomson Highway's play, *The Rez Sisters*, and from Jovette Marchessault's novel, *Mother of the Grass*, and Emma Lee Warrior's "Compatriots," Basil Johnston's "Summer Holidays in Spanish," Ruby Slipperjack's "Coal Oil, Crayons and Schoolbooks," Barry Milliken's "Run," and Daniel David Moses's "King of the Raft." These writers each organize their communities in different ways. Highway and Warrior centre their communities on reserves – the Wasaychigan Hill Indian Reserve on Manitoulin Island and the Peigan Reserve in Southern Alberta. Johnston and Slipperjack create theirs in Northern Ontario, Johnston within the confines of a Jesuit boarding school, Slipperjack in a rural village. Marchessault describes her community as a tribe living on the banks of the St. Lawrence. Milliken and Moses work with more extended and mobile communities that flow from reserves to cities and back to reserves.

All of these communities exist as intricate webs of kinship that radiate from a Native sense of family. The majority of characters in Highway's play, Marchessault's novel, Warrior's short story, and in the excerpt from Slipperjack's *Honour the Sun*, are related to one another through blood, marriage, adoption, or acceptance. While the boys at the boarding school in Basil Johnston's piece are not blood relations, Johnston shows how they band together as a family unit for identity, security, and affection, creating a communal sanctuary that offers protection from the well-meaning but assimilationist ideas of the Jesuits. Milliken and Moses define family as a Native or tribal sense of identity and place, which is maintained and carried by the characters as they move from one place to another.

This idea of community and family is not an idea that is often pursued by non-Native writers who prefer to imagine their Indians as solitary figures poised on the brink of extinction. For Native writers, community – a continuous community – is one of the primary ideas from which our literature proceeds.

While all of the stories in this collection are informed by aspects of Native culture – traditional characters, oral literature, and the idea of community – some move in other directions. Maurice Kenny's "Rain" and the selection from Joan Crate's novel, *Breathing Water*, both deal with Indians in a contemporary world, the one describing a trip to the southwest to watch the Santa Anas dance down the rain and the other describing a family living in a city. At the same time that Kenny and Crate feature Indians outside what we have come to think of as traditional roles, both writers maintain their literary connections to Native culture in part by evoking the power of the natural elements – rain, snow, hail – and by the introduction of ceremonies from Pueblo culture – the Santa Ana dancers and the rain dance – and characters from oral literature – Thunder and the Changer.

There is, I think, the assumption that contemporary Indians will write about Indians. At the same time, there is danger that if we do not centre our literature on Indians, our work might be seen as inauthentic. Authenticity can be a slippery and limiting term when applied to Native literature for it suggests cultural and political boundaries past which we should not let our writing wander. And, if we wish to stay within these boundaries, we must not only write about Indian people and Indian culture, we must also deal with the concept of "Indian-ness," a nebulous term that implies a set of expectations that are used to mark out that which is Indian and that which is not.

Of course there is no such standard, and at least three of the writers in this collection have already begun to wander past these boundaries. Beth Brant in her story, "Turtle Gal," Richard Green in "The Last Crow," and Jordan Wheeler in "The Seventh Wave" do not use traditional Native characters, nor do they make use of elements from oral literature, or create a strong sense of Native community. Instead, these writers imagine Native people engaged in a broad range of activities which do not, in and of themselves, satisfy the expectations conjured up by the notion of "Indian-ness." Beth Brant's fine story of an Indian girl who is befriended by an old, black man after her mother dies, Richard Green's slightly sardonic tale of a crow hunt, and Jordan Wheeler's humorous piece on surfing and seaside romance, do not concern themselves with "authenticity," rather they are concerned with the range of human emotions and experience that all people share. Wheeler's description of a Cree trying to learn to surf is a particularly satiric and pointed reminder that the limitations placed on us by non-Native expectations are simply cultural biases that will change only when they are ignored.

I would like to say that this collection represents a range of Native literature, because the word "range" sounds all-encompassing and important. In fact, what this anthology provides is a representational sample of the fiction that is being produced by Native writers in Canada. Given the number of Native people currently writing – and programs such as the En'owkin International School of Writing in Penticton, Native Earth Performing Arts in Toronto, De-ba-jih-mu-jig Theatre Group on Manitoulin Island, Spirit Song Native Indian Theatre Company in Vancouver, and the Saskatoon Native Theatre in Saskatoon – the potential for Native literature in the next century seems unlimited (we'll be there, you know).

In the meantime, this anthology will serve as a modest beginning, a promise of what is to come.

All my relations.

Thomas King
March 1990

▲

HARRY ROBINSON

An Okanagan Indian Becomes a Captive Circus Showpiece in England

Transcribed by Wendy Wickwire

This is about George Jim.
He belongs to Ashnola Band those days.
I had it written down, 1886.
No, I mean 1887.
That's one year I'm out there.
That's supposed to be in the 1880s.
That time, 1886,
    the people, Indians from Penticton,
        all the Okanagan Indians,
            they were sent from Similkameen.
They all move to Oroville (is now) in the month of August,
    about the last week in the month of August.
And they all get together in Oroville.
And that's when the salmon come up.
Comes up, you know, from way down.
They come up on the Colombia River
    and they come up on the Okanagan.
And some of them go up, they split up there.
Some of them go up the Columbia River.
They have a good place for catching them there in Oroville.
Kind of shallow.
Only a small river.

So, the people moved over there.
Stay there.

Put in a camp.
There is no town there yet.
There was some White people,
  they got two or three houses there.
Not many.
Then they get the salmon.
They get the salmon for,
  could be about a week or ten days.
Then the salmon keep going and go by.
They come to Osoyoos Lake
  and they follow Osoyoos Lake
    and they come to Okanagan River
      and they keep going to Okanagan Falls.
They can never go any further than Okanagan Falls.
There's a dam there.
That's as far as the salmon can go.

These Indian, when they run out of salmon,
  they know the salmon go by.
So they move.
Follow the salmon.
Then they come to Okanagan Falls.
Then the salmon can't go no more.
They were there.
They can get salmon.
Some of them died in the water and got spoiled.
Then they quit.
When they get together at Falls,
  there's a lot of Indians put in a camp.
Some of them, they play stick-game.
They kind of celebrate.
But still some of them get salmon
  at night or the daytime.
And some of them get whisky from someplace,
  from Penticton, I think.
And they drink.

And this time,
George Jim,
supposed to be a big man, stout man.
And he's a funny-looking man.
He's got short legs,
but he's pretty wide in the shoulders.
And he's got big hips.
Kinda tough-looking man.
And he was.
He's a strong man.

Then there was a White man
that lived there at Okanagan Falls.
And he's got an Indian woman from Penticton.
And they got some children,
maybe one or two.
And this White man, his name, Shuttleworth.

A lot of people drinking, you know.
And then George Jim, Shuttleworth, and some others,
they drinking at night,
and then they fighting.
But this time, that Shuttleworth,
they got beat badly by George Jim.
George Jim, he beat him almost till death.
Then, some of the boys grab him.
Because he's strong, it takes a few men to hold him.
Then they take the man who's wounded.
They take him to the camp.
They take him to the camp.
He's hurt very bad.
He's got a broken ribs
and hurt in the head, you know.
Quite a few cuts.
He hit him in the head with a club
and then he cut the skin, you know, by the club.

Not knife, but the club.
Then he kicked him in the ribs
    and his ribs were broken inside.
And then some of that bone,
    they must have gone to the lungs.
Could be.

He thought,
    "I hurt him badly
        and I might as well kill him."

So, who's going to stop him?
He's a strong man.
They went to the tepee.
Bunch of women in there,
    maybe two or three old men
        and maybe five women, old women.

So he come there and he says,
    "How's that Shuttleworth?
    I'm going to kill him if he's alive yet."
And these people told him,
    "He's dead.
    He died.
    Already died."

And they covered him with a white blanket.
He lay on the bed
    and they cover him, all his head.
And he looked like he was dead all right
    because he was covered with a white cloth.
They tell him,
    "You better stay away.
    He died.
    He dead already."

All right, he go away.

But he didn't die, that Shuttleworth.
After that he was living for about seven or eight months.
But he died just from getting beat
    because the way I see maybe the ribs they were broken
        and maybe some, they go to the lungs.
But if not go to the lungs,
    the ribs they be heal up.
They wouldn't die.
But this one here, it's bad.
Maybe it goes to the lung,
    the bone, the broken rib.

But anyway,
    George got away.
And they report that to the policeman
    because this Shuttleworth, he's a White man
        and he's got an Indian wife.
And it was reported to the police.
But the police, they couldn't get him.
Kinda scared of him because Jim,
    he's got a revolver on his hip all the time,
        and yet he's a strong man.
And the policeman, they kinda scared of him.
They just let him go.
They look for a chance to sneak to him and then get him.

So Jim, they stay away for quite a while,
    for almost one year.
About eleven months after they did that,
    that was next August
        and somebody, they cheat him.
Then they got him.
And he been down to Ashnola and Chopaka.
But they always keep away from the policeman.
They go over there and look for him,
    but they're scared of him.
They always around there but nobody get him.

They hide in the daytime in the hillside.
At night he goes to the Indian camp
    and sometimes he didn't.

Then, there was one boy, eleven years old.
And they make a lunch,
    a big lunch for Jim.
Then they told that boy,
    they told an old man,
        "You take that boy
            and show him the place
                where he can leave that lunch for Jim.
        And tell him what he's got to do.
        And tell him what he's got to say if somebody met him."
That old man used to take the lunch,
    but he's a little afraid
        maybe the policeman or some man
            might think the old man
                must have take a lunch to that wanted man.
But if the boy,
    they give him a gun, you know,
    a 22-gun, you know,
        to shoot the grouse.
And they tell him,
    "If somebody come and met you,
        if they ask you what you're doing here,
            you tell 'em,
                'I'm hunting, hunting for grouse,
                willow grouse, or rabbit, or something like that.'"

Then, he's got bags on his shoulders.
"When I get a grouse I can put it in there."
But that's where he had the lunch.
And they showed him where they can take the lunch
    and where he can leave it.
There was a big stone

and kind of hollow underneath the stone.
In the daytime they could put the lunch there.

But this man is up on the hill.
He could be watching him.
When it gets dark,
this man can come down and take the lunch
and go up the hill again.
That's Jim.
So the old man showed the boy
and tell all about what to do and what to say.
And he can take the lunch every once in a while,
every two days,
because they make a big lunch at a time.

But not long after that,
that was in the month of August, could be,
because they say that choke cherries were ripe.
They don't know if it was August or September those days.
Now I can figure myself.
When they say it's choke cherries time,
choke cherries, they ripe,
choke cherries they ripe in the month of August.
I know that.
That could be in August.
Then they were there for quite a while.

And the road gang,
they building a road.
And they call it McCurdy place.
And after that, they call it,
I forget the new man that lived there.
Anyway, McCurdy place,
that's the first man that lived there.
McCurdy for about a mile
and the river it's curved like that.
Kind of bent.
And that's where they camp, the road gang.

They had a camp there.
Those days they build a road,
    if it's far away from the town,
        they can move camp.
They got to have a camp there.
But nowadays, the workers,
    they can go from town.
It don't matter how far.
They don't put no camp.
But those days they got a camp.
They use horses, you know,
    scraper and plough to make a grade.
And they had a camp there,
    the road gang, the bunch of them.
And they had a cookhouse and a cook.
Bunch of men workers.
And there was a trail,
    but they widen out that trail to be a wagon road.
That was in 1887 then.
That was a long time ago.
No highway those days.

So the road gang was there.
And one of these boys,
    like the boss,
        maybe, the foreman, you know,
            he has to ride the horse.
No car those days,
    no motorcycle,
        no bicycle,
            no nothing.
Only saddle horse.
You know that.

Then these men
    they go to Fairview.
That's town, you know.

Mine town.
Their head boss is there.
Government.

All right,
  they went over there to see him
    and come back.
So he went over there
  and then in the afternoon, he come back from Fairview.
He went over there in the morning.
In the afternoon he come back from there.

And this George Jim,
  he took a horse and ride him around by Nighthawk.
Then they must have gone by Oroville or somewhere.
But he come back
  and he come back where that Osoyoos Road is now.

So Jim, they come on that road.
And the other one,
  that man who goes to Fairview,
    he takes the trail like from Fairview.
And they met at the top, just above Spotted Lake.

They go by Spotted Lake.
And Jim was coming on the road
  and they met there.
Then, because Jim, he's a "wanted man,"
  it was written in the government office,
    his name and how it look like and all that.
And all the White people knew that
  even if they never seen him before.
But as soon as they see him,
  they can tell that was the "wanted man."

So this man, one of the government men,
  the one that goes to Fairview,

soon as they met him,
they knew he was the one.
There was a reward, you know,
because whoever catch him is going to get paid.
Then he said to George,
They go together and they talk
and they make a good friend to one another,
and they are good friend
and it's getting late in the afternoon.
Finally they rode together
and they're getting close to the camp.
Then, it's just about suppertime then.
And this White man, he tell Jim,
"You better come with me to the camp.
Then you can eat there.
Now, it's just about suppertime."
He tell him,
"I am one of the bosses in that camp,
so you come with me
and you stay there
and after supper you can go."
And Jim, he says,
"No, I better keep going.
I can stop someplace in some of them Indians."
"Oh no. You better come.
You eat here. You'll be all right."

But you know,
when he get there,
he figure he can tell the other boys right away
and that was their judge to catch him.

So anyway,
George, he must have been hungry or something
because he stop there
and he went with that man.
And he tie up his horse.

Then,
I think this White man,
the one that's with him,
he must have tell the other ones right away.
And then he didn't know.

And then,
one of the working man,
big man, strong man,
he take the apron and he put it here.
He's not a waiter.
He's not a cook.
He's one of the ploughmen.
But he puts the apron on so he looks like a waiter, cook.
Long table
and he takes the grub
and he move over there
and he goes back and gets some more.

And Jim was sitting there
and he wanted to sit on the other side against the tent wall.
But they tell him,
"You can sit here.
Already the boys are over there."

He didn't like to sit there because it's open.

So this waiter goes by him
on his back two three times.
And then I guess these other boys,
nobody know,
they might get a club and then they hid it.
When the waiter gets over the other end of the table
and they give him that club.
Then they come back.
That was the fourth time or the fifth time
when they go by George's back.

Then this time when they go by there,
  and George was watching all the time.
They always watching.
But finally they quieten down
  and they eat.
And he's got a revolver on his hip, you know.

And when this waiter go by him,
  down it went on the back of his head
    and George just drop!
And they knocked out
  and drop off the chair.
And all the men are just on him, you know.
Bunch of men, three or four men,
  they just right on him.
And they get the rope
  and they tie their arms
  and they tie their feet.
Before he come to, he's already tied up.
They can't do nothing.
They take their gun away from him.

Then they sent one of the boys to Fairview for the policeman
  after supper, after six o'clock.
Then, whoever they went from there,
  Fairview, that's about ten or fifteen miles,
    they get there and tell the police
      and then the policemen come.
When the policemen gets there
  and they handcuff him,
  put the handcuffs on him.
Then, nothing they can do after they got the handcuffs.
They take the ropes off his feet
  and then they tell him,
    "Get on you horse."
And these policemen,
  they come on horses,

the two of them.
Then they lead him
and they tie his feet with a rope under the belly
so they could never jump off.
They got handcuffs, iron handcuffs.
They can't get away.
So they lead him to Fairview
and then they put him in jail.

Because the one,
he beat Shuttleworth.
He did.
After the six or seven months after he was beat,
he died.
He's a murderer anyway.

So, they held him in that jail for a while
and they had a trial there once or twice.
Then they take him to Penticton.
There was another court there.
Just small.
They held him there a while
and then they took him to Kamloops.
There must have been a little court in Vernon those days.
But Kamloops.
Then they had him there for a while
and then they got a sentence seven years.
Only seven years.
Take him to Westminster.

And the railroad drives into Westminster in 1886.
And they already had a railroad right in Vancouver.

And Mr. Jim,
they sent him from Kamloops on the railroad to
Westminster.
And then they had him in that penitentiary.

And he was in there three years.
Supposed to be seven years and then he'll come out.
That's his sentence.
Seven years.

He was in jail three years
    and one night toward morning,
    about two o'clock in the morning then
        because all the cells, you know,
            whoever's in the cell, maybe one or two,
                the policeman lock 'em.
Then in the morning they could open 'em.
Unlock 'em.
But Jim was locked.
All alone in one cell.
But toward morning,
    about two o'clock in the morning,
        somebody open that.
They got a key,
    open the door,
        and they come in.
There's three of them – policemen.
They got the clothes, uniform – guards.
Those days, the policemen,
    they haven't got no uniform.
But the guards, they got some kind of a uniform.

So, the three of them come in.
And Jim, he wake up.
Still in bed.
They told him,
    "Jim, you get up and put your clothes on.
    We come and get you."

I'm not sure if it was three.
I think it's only two.
But the driver, that makes three.

They got a driver on the buggy out there.
But these two,
    they're both guards,
        go in and tell Jim,
            "You dress up and we come and get you.
            There's a buggy outside with a driver.
            You get on the buggy
                and we all get on
                    and we go to Vancouver.
            Early in the morning,
                the train is going to leave Vancouver.
            We got to go on the train.
            We move you.
            There's one jail a long way from here.
            We move you.
            You're going to be over at that jail.
            Long ways from here.
            You leave this place."

Well what can he say,
    because this is the policeman, guard, you know.
He has to do whatever they tell him.
All right, he dress up and he went out.
There was a buggy there
    and he get on the buggy
        and they all get on the buggy
            and they go to Vancouver early in the morning.

Now, they got a different time.
Now, they leave there eight o'clock in the evening from
    Vancouver.
But at that time it might have been in the morning.
Might be four o'clock in the morning
    or something like that.

Anyway,
    early in the morning they get on the train

and they went.
And they going all day and all night
and all day and all night again.
And Mr. Jim, he thinks,
"By God, that was a long way.
I wonder where they take me."

They take him into where they eat, you know,
on the train.
And he got a chance to ask the waiter.
I guess the policemen went back,
and just only himself.
And he asked the waiter,
and the waiter told him,
"They take you to Halifax.
Then there, you're going to take the boat from Halifax to England."

So, they find that out,
but what have they go to say?
So anyway, they get him to Halifax.
Then they told him,
"We're going to be here for a while.
We're waiting for the boat."
Because those days
it takes the boat a month to go over the seas to England.
One month.
But now it's only about four days.
So they wait there about four or five days.
Then the boat came.
Then they put him in the boat,
the whole bunch.
These two, they always along with him,
the same man.

So, they mention that.
They see one Indian in England

and they told him,
this Indian from Enderby,
not Indian altogether,
but he speak in Okanagan.
So, he says he went on the water.
They could see the mountains, the ground,
for one week and no more.
Two weeks,
never see nothing but water.
Then he see again a little ridge.
Little ground.
One week and then they landed.
Then from there
they took him on the buggy
or on the train or something for quite a ways.
Then they leave him there.
But not in jail no more.
They give him a good house.
a good big house,
big room,
good bed.
They feed him good
and then they kept him.

They watch him all the time.
But once in a while they took him
and put him on the train
and they went away.
They stay away for two or three months
and then come back.
That was his home place.
In two months or more,
they come back to England
and they stay there for two or three weeks,
maybe one month,
then they took him to another direction.
That's in European somewhere.

They took him everywhere for show.
Whenever they get somewhere
  and there'd be a big forum
    and table or something.
Then they tell him to get up there
  and walk around there.
Then, the people in the big room,
  big house chock-full of people,
    and he watching them.
And these people, they pay.
Pay money to see that Indian.
There is no Indian in Europe at that time.
Only him.

So the White people, they make money out of him.
And he was there four years.

And this man from Enderby,
  he's a half-breed.
His name, Charlie.
Charlie Harvie, his name.
He talks in Okanagan.
He's half-breed.
And he don't say,
  but I think myself he must be in the army,
    that Charlie,
      because he went and he get to England.
Then he come back from England
  and he came home to Enderby.
And when he got home,
  he said when he was in England,
  he said, there's a big bunch of boys,
    all young boys just like he was,
      just like his age.
Bunch of them and they were there.

So one of these boys told him,
  asked him where he come from.

And he said he came from the Okanagan, British Columbia.
Okanagan.
Then, they told him,
  "There was a man not far from here,
  he is supposed to come from Okanagan, British Columbia.
  He is supposed to speak in your language.
  Maybe we should take you over there
    and then you can see that man."

Then, he said,
  "No, I don't like to go because,"
    (see, he's got a boss, he must be an army man)
  "my boss they may not like it that way."
So, the other boss says,
  "Your boss, he's not going to know that.
  We take you over there.
  We're not going to tell your boss.
  You're going to see that man."

All right,
  so they went.
The boys took him over there.
Then they get to that place
  and they go in to where that Jim was.
That's his house.
Then the boys told him,
  "This man, he speak in your language."
Then the both of them started to speak in Okanagan.

Not only one.
They went over there two or three times
  to see him and visit him
    for quite a while.

And Jim,
  they told him all about what they have done
    and so on.

And then they took him from Westminster
  and they took him on the train a long ways
    and they put him on the boat for one month.
Then they had him there.
  "Then they take me out from here a long ways.
  I don't know which way,
    but they take me out a long ways.
    Wherever I stop, a lot of men get in there.
    Then they make me walk around on the boards.
    High.
    Then I walk around and all the people look at me.
    Then I go.
    We go to another place.
    A lot of places.
    In one month or two months
      we come back.
    And this is my home place."

But he says,
  "Charlie, when you get back to British Columbia,
    you can go from Enderby to Ashnola."
Right in Ashnola he's got an aunt and uncle.
And he said to Charlie,
  "You could tell my uncle or my aunt
  to see if they can come and get me.
  They got a lot of money.
  They got a lot of cattle.
  They got enough money.
  They should come and get me.
  In another way they can talk to the Indian agent.
  And then the Indian agent can contact to Ottawa,
    to the Indian Affairs.
  Then, whoever's coming to get me,
    their fare can be paid that way.
  But maybe they'll have a little money with them anyway.
  But my people, they're well-off.

They should do that and come and get me."

So Charlie, he said,
"I will when I get home."

And about a year after that,
Charlie came back.
Come back to Enderby.
They stay there almost one year after they come back.
And then they ride on the saddle horse all the way to Ashnola.
Then they see that John, his name was,
and Mary.
They are cousins.
That's Jim's aunt, that Mary,
and his uncle, John.
He told them all about contact the Indian agent and to Ottawa
and to all that.
And he said,
"If you want me,
I can be with you because I can speak in English,
you know."

But these Indians, they couldn't understand.
They don't know.
In another way, they don't like it.

They say,
"They should not pay for our fare
because that's a lot of money."
They figure they could pay for their own fare
but it takes a lot of money.
And they could never understand about the contact
so they could get paid their fare from the Indian affairs.
Charlie told them,
but they couldn't understand.
Charlie, he was waiting around,
but he said,

"If you need me, I come back and help you,
or else I can go with you for interpreter over there
to get that man back."

But they just dismissed.
No more.
They never get him.

But, before they find out he was alive yet
at the time when they took Jim from Westminster,
took him away,
then they rode from the jail to John.
He was a chief, you know.
And he told John that
"Jim was in jail here
but he died and we bury him."

But he not die.
They take him away.

So they think his people,
they just got to know he died and that's all.
But they decided they should come and get the body.
Take it out and bring him home.
So they did.
They come, that John and Mary and some others.
They got an interpreter, you know,
who can speak in English.
Then they come on horseback with the packhorses to Hope.
Then they talk to the people in Hope
and they tell them,
"You can't leave your horses here.
There's no feed for the horses.
You have to go to Chilliwack
and then you can put your horses in there with
the Indians.
There's all kinds of feed there for horses.

And then you can take the boat from Chilliwack to
Westminster."

So, they did.
They did get to Westminster
and they go to the jail office
and they tell him,
"We're coming to get George Jim."
"He's already buried here."
So, they said,
"Yeah, we talk to one another.
We'll see.
Just wait a while, a couple of days."

Then, they talk to one another
and they find out what to say about him.
Then they say,
"All right, we know.
This is the one right there in the graveyard.
We can dig him.
We dig him out and we clean 'em and we change the coffin.
Then you guys can take him on the boat as far as Chilliwack
and then you could put him on the packhorse."

Well, it's in a box
because they could pack the horse on each side of
something.
Then they could put the box crossways
all the ways from Chilliwack to Ashnola.
Then they did that
and they take him out and clean him
and put medicine on him
so he wouldn't be smell.
Change the coffin and seal it
and told him not to open it.
"Don't open it
because we give him medicine.

But in the box he's not cold.
They might be kinda smell,
but by the time you get it over there,
not to open 'em."

All right, they bring 'em
and they never open 'em.
But when they get him to Ashnola,
then, whoever they were there,
and they say,
"We should open 'em.
We should make sure if that was him."
"Well," these other people said,
"if he's going to be smelly, that don't matter.
Open 'em, we want to see."
So, they break it open and they looked at 'em.
"That's not Jim. That was a Chinaman."
Kinda stout Chinaman.
He must have been in jail.

They can't take him back, so they bury him there.
They were around there for a while
and they thought maybe they make a mistake over there.
"We better go again to get Jim.
They might mistake.
Maybe Jim is still there."

They went again
and they get there
and they told him,
"This is not Jim you give us.
This is a Chinaman."
"By gosh, that's too bad.
We made a mistake.
We know that.
We find that out,
but you fellas are gone.

George is THERE.
Now that you've come back,
we can take him out and clean him
and you can take him away.
Take him home."

They do the same thing.
Dug him out, clean him, put medicine on him
and changed the box,
and tell him not to open it.

So, they bring him,
and that was the second time.
From Westminster to Chilliwack.
Then, they packed him from Chilliwack to Ashnola.
When they get there,
whoever they were home tell 'em,
"We got to open 'em, see,
to make sure if it was Jim.
Maybe another Chinaman."

Anyhow, they open 'em.
They looked at him
and he was a Negro boy.
A small man too.

Well, they bury him there.
But there's no use to go back and get George.

And George is not dead.
They take him away.

Then later on, a few years after that,
and Charlie Harvie come back from England.
Then he ride over there and he tell them about it.

Long time, quite a few years after that,

and then they find out
George Jim, he's not dead.
He's alive yet, but he's in England.

So, that's the end of the story.

RUBY SLIPPERJACK

Coal Oil, Crayons and Schoolbooks

Fall 1962

The radio is on, playing country music, and Mom hums over the noise of the splattering bacon grease on the stove. It's nice and warm inside in the soft lamplight. I smell the bacon and coffee. I stretch and yawn, kicking my blanket off.

Mom glances at me and says, "Go out first and I'll have your breakfast on the table when you come back."

I jump off the top bunk and slip my black rubber boots on and dash out the door. I slow to a walk when the cold, damp air hits me in the face. I can't even see anything. No island, no Aunty's cabin, no outhouse. What a weird feeling. Like I'm the only person in the whole world; white mist all around me. It's like standing on a tiny island with just naked branches all around me and no noise, just my heart beating and the sound of my chattering teeth. I'm cold. I walk briskly toward the outhouse.

Coming back, I can smell the wood smoke from the stovepipe and the bacon. Once I reach the porch, I dash into the cabin. "Hey, Mom. I can't see a thing out there. Our cabin has floated off somewhere by itself into a big white cloud."

She smiles at me and says, "Sit down and be quiet. The others are still sleeping." I gulp down the bacon strips in thick, soft slices of bannock. Mom is shutting down the stove and turning down the lamps. She's putting on her boots and thick coat.

"Where you going? Can I come with you?" I ask between mouthfuls. She glances around at the sleeping bodies on the bed and smiles. "Sure. But finish eating first. We'll go and check the fishnet by the island." I quickly wash down my last mouthful with the sweet creamed coffee and rush to put my coat on.

Softly, Mom closes the door behind us and we go down to the shore. It's getting a lot brighter but the fog is still pretty thick over the water. The noises seem to amplify in the stillness as we turn the canoe over and into the water. I get in first, then Mom gets in, pushing the canoe off with her foot. In the stillness, the drip and swirl of the water over our paddles is very loud and clear. I breathe deeply, holding my paddle still for a moment. Mom also stops and the only sound is the gurgle of water at the front of the canoe. My coat swishes against my arm when I turn to give Mom a smile and then we paddle on again.

The morning train comes early in the morning now. We can hear the screech of the wheels and the *sh-sh-sh-sh*, when it stops. We're at the west end of the island. We drift a few feet before Mom lifts the lead rope with her paddle and starts pulling us alongside the net, lifting it out of the water at each arm's length.

The train pulls out, moving faster with each roar of its engine. Its click-clack sound grows fainter down the tracks.

There's one fish, a large trout. Then another, and another one! The fourth one is a slimy, old catfish. Mom throws him back in the water. She swishes the net in the water a few times, washing out the slime before we move forward again. There are no more fish. She drops the net back in the water.

I hear a door shut. "Look." I point. "Who's that?" The fog has partially lifted and I see someone coming out of our cabin! The figure walks down the road.

Puzzled, Mom says, "I don't know." Then she shrugs. "If he's someone who's just gotten off the train, he'll come back later."

We paddle toward home. I smell wood smoke. People have gotten up and started their fires. I like the morning smell. Mom looks pleased with the trout piled at her feet. We can see a shadow inside the cabin moving across the window. It must be Jane looking for her socks. I've got them on. Anyway, I have to put on my long stockings for school, so I'll just tell her I kept them warm for her.

The lake has gone down a bit. I can tell because a rock, which used to be underwater, sticks out by our boat landing. I hop onto it now and pull the canoe to the shore. I hold the canoe steady while Mom steps out on a rock. "Get a knife and pan for me," she says, reaching for the trout.

I run up and dash into the cabin. Everyone's awake and eating breakfast at the table. "Lazy bones and sleepy heads!" I say to them, whipping out the dishpan.

Grabbing the knife, I dash down the lake to Mom. She's already pulled the canoe up and turned it over. The early morning sun is slowly drying up the mist. Mom looks up at the sky. "It will be a cool, clear day, today. Go and get dressed for school now."

The old man next door comes out and heads for his outhouse. I know one of Mom's trout will be going to them. Reluctantly, I leave Mom cleaning the fish and walk back to the cabin, bursting now with the sound of sharp voices and clattering dishes.

Brian and Tony are arguing. I push the door open, just in time to see a wet shirt fly over the table and smack the side of Jane's head. Brian clamps a hand over his mouth before blurting out, "Sorry. I was trying to hit Tony. That's his shirt."

Jane picks up the shirt off the floor while Tony is bending over, laughing. Suddenly, Jane's foot shoots out and boots Tony squarely in his pants and flings the shirt at him. "Hang up your shirt, you!"

I glance at her, wondering what's eating her? Quickly pulling the socks off, I decide not to say anything about them. I've already changed my clothes when Mom comes in with the three fish, their dark, shiny backs curved inside the pan.

"Where's the comb, Mom?" She reaches up high on the top dish shelf. "How is anyone going to find it when you hide it way up there?" I ask.

"If I didn't, I wouldn't know where to look for it when you ask, would I?" she answers.

Smiling, I sit down on the bench and tug at the tangles in my hair. The door opens and in comes a man with grey hair jutting out from the side of the dark green cap on his head. But it's the sparkling eyes and the smiling face that brings a thrill of excitement, love and respect; it's the Medicine Man.

He surveys the room with joy on his face. His eyes laugh into mine and my face stretches into a wide smile. Mom rushes by me and ushers our visitor to the table where she promptly makes breakfast for him. He is the one we saw walking away from the cabin after the train left. He lives far away in a town by the train tracks. He comes when someone calls him for medicine and he usually stays at our place. Now he says Rita's mother called him. Mom reminds him that our canoe is there when he needs it. He usually goes off to gather the plants he uses.

Oh, I hate to leave. Sometimes I don't understand some of the things they're talking about, but I could listen to him talk all day. How I wish I could follow him around, and find out what he does and see how he makes his medicinal brews.

"Are you finished? I need the comb." Maggie is poking me in the back. I hand the comb over my shoulder to her. He has a strange accent. He's not from around here, that's for sure.

Jane walks by and grumbles, "Where are my socks? I couldn't find those socks anywhere this morning."

Feeling a bit guilty, I point to the laundry box in the corner. "I saw them in there."

Mom announces, "It's almost time for school," and glances at the clock on the shelf.

I linger as long as I can as I put my coat on. Finally, I blurt out, "Are you going to be here when I come back for lunch?"

The Medicine Man chuckles and winks at me. "Yes, I'll make sure I get back in time to see you at lunch." I smile broadly and dash off.

The sun is shining on the sides of the cabins now, but the tall weeds and twigs are still very wet. I run as fast as I can through the bush path, my shortcut to school. I emerge behind the schoolhouse. The teacher is just coming out of the school with the bell. He usually hands the bell to one of the kids to ring it but there isn't anyone outside yet. He glances at his watch and smiles at me. "Good morning! Would you like to ring the bell this morning?"

I smile and shake my head, "No."

He glances at his watch again, then starts ringing the bell, ding-dong, ding-dong. Giggling, I step up to him and say, "Everyone's going to go to church."

Misunderstanding me, he asks, "Right now? Is the minister here?"

I giggle again, pointing at the bell. "You ring it like the church bell. Everyone's going to go to church instead." He throws back his dark, curly head and laughs. Encouraged, I continue, "You have to ring it faster to make it sound like a school bell!" Smiling down at me, he shakes the bell, ting-a-ling-a-ling. I nod and smile, "Now it sounds like a school bell."

I stand around by myself for about a minute before the kids come scurrying in from all directions. The teacher stands on the wooden steps, as the kids jostle each other into two crooked lines. When Teacher finally satisfies himself that there are indeed two lines, he flings the door open and, one by one, we troop in.

The smell of coal oil permeates the room, almost blanketing the smell of crayons and schoolbooks. We hang our jackets and coats on the tinkling hangers and kick off our boots and shoes. The one-room school now echoes with the sound of chattering voices, scraping chairs and shuffling feet.

Order and quiet follow the teacher's steps from the back of the room to the front. Roll call brings forth cries of "present," "present," "present." I recall my kindergarten days when it took me a while to figure out what "present" meant. All I knew was that it's what you had to say when your name was called. Suddenly, all is quiet. Then I notice all eyes are glued on me. Teacher repeats my name! Startled, I quickly answer, "Present!" Amidst the giggles and twitters, I bury my burning face into my book.

Like a sponge, I soak up the words from the teacher, but I get bored when it comes to writing it all down. I love the stories in our English lesson. I always leaf through the book far ahead, sometimes to the end when I'm supposed to be writing. Jed pokes me and points at Liza's back. A big louse is making its way down her back. What if it falls on my desk. Then I feel the teacher brush my arm as he walks by. My eyes widen when his hand hovers for a second on Liza's back. He bends to correct her on a word and moves away again. The bug is gone! Those of us who notice, watch him make his way to the stove while talking about the chapter we've just read. His hand stops for a second over the stove top before he continues, slowly circling the room talking and explaining. Jed and I glance at each other, smiling.

An awful smell keeps getting worse. Soon the kids are giggling again. It's Ben's stinky feet. Then Cousin Joe leans back and stretches; a fresh burst of laughter erupts. His big toe is sticking out of a hole in his sock. I giggle into my hand so hard, it makes a snorting noise. I'm about to burst.

Then quickly the laughter dies when Teacher stands up from his desk and stares at each of us with that look that says "No more." Heads down, we continue with our work. Finally, he says, "Books away! Fifteen minutes for recess outside."

With sighs of relief we leave, one row at a time, coats and boots on and out the door. Laughing and squealing as we chase each other around the school and the swings. Actually, I think Cousin Joe is mad at me for laughing at him. Teacher is coming out with the basketball. He plays with the boys all the time, so I head for the swings. Rita and I decide to sit together on one seat. Since I'm bigger, she sits on top of my lap with her legs on each side of me. Who will push us now? Oh no! Here comes Cousin Joe for his revenge. I can see his face . . . Suddenly, Teacher calls, "Joe! Catch!"

The ball comes flying and Joe catches it and drops it to the ground. He kicks it, right smack in Tommy's face. That's John Bull's son. Tommy sets up howling. Blood gushes from his nose and runs down the front of his shirt. Quickly, Teacher ushers Tommy into the school. Now, a thought has just occurred to me: I grin, thinking I could threaten to tell John Bull on Cousin Joe if he comes after me again. Teacher comes out and blows the whistle; it's time to go in.

Still giggling, Rita, Maggie, and I stay at the end of the lineup for the cup of milk and large vitamin biscuit. Yuck. It's powdered milk mixed in warmish water and the biscuits taste like old socks. I tuck my biscuit under my waistband; Rosiak likes them. Jumbo won't eat it though; he makes that face and drops it on the ground.

I watch Ben, Jed, and some others asking for more biscuits and I realize that it is probably their breakfast.

It's back to lessons; this time, with math on the chalkboard. I like writing on the board; if only the others didn't have to see it. I'm always afraid of making a mistake for all to see. Whenever someone makes a mistake, everyone starts laughing. I feel a hand tuck my hair back over my shoulder and I glance up to smile at Teacher. He looks at my sketch of Rosiak and Jumbo on the corner of my book. I quickly put my hand over it. He continues down the aisle. I smell crayons and plasticine from the little kids by the window. Brian and Tony are whispering quite loudly. It seems like such a short time before Teacher says, "Time to put your books away. It's lunchtime."

Noise and activity fill the room again as we leave. I run as fast as I can through my shortcut home. The dry brown leaves crackle and swish under my feet. The air is crisp and cool. A flood of joy fills me as I dash into the clearing. Our cabin door is open; smoke is coming up in blue wisps and I hear voices and laughter.

I skip across the porch and stand at the open door as the Medicine Man turns from the stove – "Oh, there you are. So did you learn something new this morning?"

I nod, "Yep."

He stands by the stove, stirring a pot of strong-smelling stuff on the stove. He grins at me. "Don't worry, you won't have to eat this for lunch."

I giggle and sit down at the table where Mom dishes out boiled trout and potatoes. Oh, I'm hungry! Then Brian and Tony come running in, panting, with Maggie right behind them.

Jane seems to be in a better mood and she hovers over us to pick up the dirty dishes. She does not go to school; she's too old to start.

After lunch I ask the Medicine Man, "Would you give me some medicine, too?"

"Oh? And what's the matter?" he asks.

"I have a very sore arm. It hurts!" I gasp, holding my arm.

He takes my arm and turns it over examining it. "Did you fall down? How did you hurt it?" he asks.

"No, I didn't fall down. I've been writing and writing all morning and my arm is very sore now." I groan.

He chuckles and Mom sends me off to wash my face and hands. I sit and listen to him again, watching him take so much care of the pot on the stove. Finally, Mom says it's time for us to go back to school again. The Medicine Man is going back on the train this afternoon, so I won't see him again.

I pause at the door and say, "Goodbye."

He gives me a big smile, saying, "I'll tell my wife that the trout I'm taking home is from The Owl. I saw you checking the fishnet with your mother this morning."

I turn and run down the path, embarrassed that he called me by my family nickname. The Owl; what a silly name!

The boys are already there when I approach the school. Teacher comes out of his house and falls into step beside me. I'm embarrassed. I slow down, as I look at his shirt. He has mud on his sleeve from the ball. Hey, that's the shirt he had on his clothesline on Saturday. Aunty and I were coming around the corner of the store when she started giggling and pointing at the teacher's house. Then I noticed the most jolly and cheerful-looking clothes I have ever seen on a clothesline. The shirt was bouncing and swinging in the breeze, hanging by its wrist cuffs. The collar was pinned straight across by half a dozen clothespins. One minute it would do chin-ups, the next, forward swings.

And his pants were hanging over the clothesline by the knees, swinging back and forth, doing occasional sit-ups. The socks were dancing and flipping on their own individual pins. And his shorts, oh, Aunty nearly died laughing. The shorts were hung, flat as you please, with about four pins straight across the waist . . . I can feel my face burning at the thought. Aunty had said, "No modesty at all!"

People usually use one pin on the back or side of the underpants, so they won't hang so obviously. And, right between his shorts, hung his dish-towels. Aunty told it all to Mom when we got home and they all laughed so hard, I started to feel sorry for Teacher.

He stands facing me. "Huh?" I ask.

"Say 'pardon me.'"

Oh, oh, I can feel a giggle swelling in my chest, I swallow it down.

He continues, thoughtfully, "I said that you have a very expressive face when you're looking at me." His eyes twinkle with amusement. I look at him totally confused. I have no idea what he's talking about. He guides me ahead and rubs my head with his hand, saying, "Oh, never mind."

We resume walking toward the boys. And then it starts; I knew it from their faces. They tease me about the teacher. In our language, they chant, "Teacher likes her-er; Teacher likes her-er."

I ignore them and begin going out of my way to avoid the teacher. I no longer speak to him outside the school and I always wait till lots of kids are in front of the school, so I can stand at the back of the line.

It is a very slow afternoon. After recess, I watch the same kids stock up on the vitamin biscuits and milk again. They probably won't have another meal till tomorrow's recess. Once back at our seats, I hear Cousin Joe say loudly, "Hey, Ben! Why don't you go for a walk in the water with your socks on before the water freezes?"

Ben promptly answers, "Aw, shut up! We can see your toe, but we wouldn't see any brains sticking out if I put a hole in your head!"

The whole class roars with laughter. Of course, we all speak our own language, so after surveying the class, Teacher raps a ruler on the desk and says, "Joe, Ben, save it till after school, eh?"

In quiet titters, we resume our work on the books, I hear the train coming. That's the one the Medicine Man is getting on. I imagine him boarding the train, the conductor getting back on behind him, the door clanging shut and some delay . . . maybe he dropped his fish and had to get down to pick it up again. Oh, there it goes; I can hear the roar of the engine as the train pulls out.

Finally, the time comes to go home. It's after school and, without looking back, I dash out of the door and straight through the bushes on my shortcut. The door is closed. As I near the cabin, I can see the padlock on the door. A grip of panic seizes me. I stop and listen – no sound. "Mom!" I yell. "Mom!"

Wandering toward the canoe, I smell something I've smelled before. It's tanning smoke. I can see the smoke drifting over the bay now. I dash down the path behind the cabin toward the lake. Behind a windscreen by the lake, Mom kneels in front of a long roll of moose hide, suspended over a pot of smoking sticks. I like the smell. With a big smile, I kneel down beside her and watch spirals of thick smoke escaping from the numerous stitches along the seams of the hide.

With a sigh of contentment and happiness, I turn to watch the lake, so dark and so cold. Mom squints against the smoke to peek through a hole and plug it up again. A few wisps of curly hair have escaped the cotton kerchief over her head.

We hear Brian, loudly yelling, "Mom! Mom!"

Grinning, I look at Mom and ask, "If I was that loud, how come you didn't answer me?"

She looks at me with a smile. "I figured I'd just see if that button nose of yours works!"

I laugh. "Oh, it works all right. I had to put up with the stinky smell of Ben's feet all day long!"

She hands me the keys and says, "Go open the door and make sure you leave the keys in the lock and put them away on the very top shelf, understand?"

I nod and grab the keys. Feeling quite important, I unlock the door and fling it wide for Brian and Tony. Maggie is just getting home. "Where's Jane?" I ask.

She shrugs and says, "How should I know? You got home first!" Then we both remember at the same time. Their father came yesterday and asked Jane to go with him to his trapline this winter. We both dash out the door, around the corner toward Mom.

"Hey, Mom! Where's Jane? Is she going or not?" I ask.

Mom is putting her things away. She looks at Maggie and answers, "No, she's not going with your father. But, right now, she's with your mother. Your mother got off the train this afternoon. Go and see her before I get supper ready."

Maggie sighs, "No, I don't want to see her. When's supper? I'm hungry."

"Is your stomach all you ever think about?" asks Jane, as she comes up behind us, smiling at Maggie.

Mom looks toward the house, as she shakes out and hangs the freshly smoked hide on the line. Who's kicking the door? Walking behind them toward the cabin, I feel a knot develop in my stomach.

There, at the door, stands Brian. All eyes now fall on the shiny padlock securely locking the door. Brian sheepishly looks at his feet when the kicks come again from the inside. "Tony's got the key," Brian murmurs.

Feeling sick, I refuse to look at Mom. I feel her eyes on me. Jane sits down on the steps to wait for someone to figure out something. My mind is scrambling, but I can't think of a crack big enough to slip the key through. Mom has already sealed the windows and reinforced the boards all around the door.

I hear Maggie ask, "Is the stove cold?"

Mom nods, "I didn't add anymore wood after lunch." She glances at the chimney pipe sticking out on the side of the roof. I'm missing something here. Nothing more is said as Mom gets a length of string from the woodpile and ties a small rock to the end. Maggie has scrambled up the log ends at the corner of the cabin and crawls along the edge of the roof to the stovepipe and Mom throws her the string. Mom calls through the door, "Tony? Look inside the stove. Maggie is letting down a string. Take the rock off and tie the key on."

We can hear the stove lid banging open. Maggie's laughter echoes down the stovepipe. Soon Maggie swings the key on the end of the string down to Mom.

Without a word or glance at me, Mom unlocks the door and they all go in. I sit down on the porch steps, wishing Little Dog was still alive; he got hit by the train before Wess left. Jumbo doesn't play anymore and Rosiak is always the proper, dignified lady. There are no more birds on the island and everything is peaceful, quiet . . . and cold.

BARRY MILLIKEN

Run

"Uhnee-peesh mah?" my mother asks. She has been watching me since I came downstairs, and, now that I have eaten, she knows that I'm going.

"Up the road," I say. That is all I tell her because that is all I know. She doesn't say anything for a minute, just stands by the noisy old wash machine looking grumpy and feeding wet clothes into the wringer. Her hair is tied by a rubber band at the back, but many strands are loose and hang like little droopy antennas beside her face. I see many lines that weren't there before my father died. In her eyes there is sadness that makes me mad when I see it, just like everything seems to do lately. I know what she is going to say next, and I turn away as she does.

"When you gonna be back?"

For a minute I stand like that, with my back to her, feeling suddenly like I want to cry. But I am fifteen, so I will not.

"Peter?"

A loud bump, and then my sister's laughing comes from above me. The made feeling gets worse. I shrug my shoulders.

"Are you going to Budge's?"

I shrug again and hear her sigh; I know that some of the sadness in her eyes is because of me.

"If you're going to Budge's, I want you to take something to her."

Finally, I turn halfway around and nod.

She goes to the cupboard, and, from the edge of my vision, I see her reach up to the top shelf. My sister's baby starts to cry in her high chair. My mother comes to me and holds out her hand. Without looking up, I take the thing and shove it into my back pocket.

"Don't forget," she says. I turn and go, feeling her eyes on me. As I reach the front door, I think I hear her say my name, but, when I turn, she has gone into the kitchen and I hear the high chair bang as she lifts the baby from it.

Out on the porch, I can see, without looking, the mess of beer bottles and cigarette butts around me on the floor. After the washing, and after the baby is cleaned up, my mother will come like a servant woman and clean up this mess my sister and her friends made last night. Her and Tucker.

Above me, the clouds look like blankets, dark and light, a big unmade bed.

In front of the house is Tuck's car, which sits exactly as he left it yesterday about four o'clock. That's when he and my sister's friends arrived. All around it the ground is bare and oily, littered with tools, flattened old cigarette packages, beer bottles from other days and yesterday. The trunk and one door are open. On a table beside the car there is part of a carburetor and beside this Sacha, our cat, is sprawled. As I come down the porch steps, she gets up yawning and stretching. A car comes along the road and stops in a big cloud of dust. It backs up, then comes up our laneway with the wheels spinning, throwing dirt and stones behind it and sending Sacha running. I recognize who it is before the car comes to a stop about three feet from Tuck's. They are two of his friends, Manny and Sly. One look and I know they have been drinking all night. Manny's eyes are only half open, as he tilts his head out the window.

"Hey Pee-pee," he says and leans his head back on the seat. His mouth is twisted into a half-smile, and he looks about ready to pass out.

"C'mere."

When I go up beside the car, he lifts his arm and lets it rest along the top of the door. In his hand is a half-full bottle of beer.

"Wanna drink?"

I say no and stare at a tattoo he has put on his arm himself, the shape of a star with letters at the points. With his head still back, he squints up at me.

"Where's Tuck?"

I look toward the lake and shrug my shoulders.

"Sleeping, I guess," I say.

He repeats the word "sleeping" so softly I can hardly hear it. His eyes close, and, for a minute, I think he is gone. But, then, in a voice louder and harder, he says:

"Don't you know?"

His eyes half open and fix on me. There is white stuff around the corners of his mouth.

"Nope," I say, and bend forward, letting a gob of spit fall to the ground beside the car. For a minute again his eyes close and he says nothing, then when I glance down I see a little smile has come to his face.

"Hey Pee-pee, I hear you're a fast runner."

His smile gets bigger. "'Nother fug'n Longboat, I hear."

I shrug and say nothing. Sly laughs from his side of the car, and Manny rolls his head to look at him.

"'Nother fug'n Longboat," he says again.

They laugh harder. I turn and walk away and see the black shape of my dog back along the tree-line. He stops and looks up when I whistle and comes toward me as I start to trot along the path leading south from home. Manny calls out something, and Sly's laughing reaches me like high, strange barking, pushing me faster. Boog comes jumping through the high grass and reaches the road the same time as me. There is dust and pieces of dry grass on his black fur. Once free of the grass, he leaps high beside me, then runs ahead. He will stop and sniff around a tree or pole until I pass, then run on again. He was a present from my father for my tenth birthday. Now he's the best friend I have.

At first, as I run, the road feels hard; I hear my feet on the gravel which lies along both sides. There are bumps in the middle where I never go except to cross, and now I find the smooth part which lies just beside the gravel. My feet under me go faster; the air hits harder, cleaning me, crashing away the sound behind me.

Because it is Sunday morning, there is no one around and no cars in sight. The lake on my right doesn't sparkle the way it does when the sun is out, but it doesn't matter. I fall into a good pace, and I know that soon nothing will matter. The ground lies out flat and straight, my feet flash under me, and I am filled with something that washes everything else away. It is a power that makes me know that when I run I am strong, and there is nobody who is better. That's the way it has been since the first time the strangeness happened nearly two years ago when I had just turned fourteen.

People were just starting to notice how fast and far I could run, although I hadn't yet raced against Simon Cloud, who was known to be the fastest runner on the reserve.

An older boy bet me that I couldn't run from his place, out to the highway and back, in less than an hour. I told him I had no money to bet, but I knew, too, that I hesitated because I wasn't sure I could do it. The distance he talked about was four and a half miles each way. I had never gone more than six miles without a rest, and never against a clock. I also knew that my mother wouldn't want me getting into something like that. Nine miles without a rest. It scared me all right. But the more I thought about it, the more I wanted to try it.

Carman Fisher was there, and, rather than see a good bet go down the drain, he covered the other boy's money, then told me that if I could do it, I'd get ten dollars.

It was very hot that day, and fifteen minutes after I started I was wishing that I had put it off till evening. But I found a pace that I knew I could keep until at least the halfway point, and, although it seemed like an hour before I reached the highway, someone yelled as I started back that twenty-four minutes were gone.

I had done better than I thought, but now as I ran the sun seemed like a torch that hung too close above me, the roar stonier than I ever remembered it. I knew that it was because I was afraid. Please God, I said inside, don't let me fail and shame myself. Don't let it happen that they laugh at me.

But, as I ran, my arms and legs went away from me and became only things I saw faintly, at the edges of my vision. My breath became a useless noise that flew in and out of my open mouth. Sweat flew from me and into my eyes, until I had to close them. Please, I said again. Then ahead of me the road blurred and a brightness flashed that seemed to go into me like a shock, and suddenly, not as much in vision, but in feeling as strong as the flash of light had been, my father was there, around me, in me. The tiredness was gone, the road and the air helped me again. But more than that was the joy I felt that my father had come back to me.

All I knew about Carman Fisher before I made that run was that he was about three years older than me, he had a car, and he worked at the lumberyard in town. After that day, he'd honk his horn if he passed me on the road, or sometimes he'd stop and talk a little.

One day he asked it I'd like to go for a ride. I felt important and honoured to be considered a friend by someone who was working and had his own car. We went to the beach where he met some people he knew – older kids, like him. When they offered him a beer, he said, "I hope you got one for my buddy here. We're gonna be watchin' him in the Olympics one day." Everybody laughed, but Carman looked at me and winked as if to say, "You'll show 'em."

The beer made me feel good, almost like when I run.

After that I didn't see him for a long time, then I heard he had found a job in the city and was living there.

It was around then that the trouble at home started. When my father died, he took something that had made everything good for our family. After he was gone, we couldn't seem to talk, but instead, as if like dogs, we each took our sorrow to a different part of the house, not willing to share it.

My sister quit school and started going with Tuck, who is a good-for-nothing drunk. The next thing I knew, he was living with us and sharing my sister's bed every night. She had a child one year after my father died. The boy is a symbol of the shame she has brought to our family. He cries and messes, and it is my mother who sees to him, and cooks the meals, and cleans up.

"We need the money Glenda gives me," she says. "You want us to live on welfare?"

I want to tell her that it wouldn't be any worse to have that shame than it is to have the shame of living the way we are. At least then she'd be able to tell them to get out. But of course I don't say it, because I know she wouldn't do it. That's the real shame. She has let it happen. She has betrayed my father. And that's why I have to go. Now, as I run, I have decided. I will do what has been in the back of my mind to do for a long time. It's a good day for running and I have a good start. Almost fifty miles to the city, almost two marathons.

Something I remember, too, makes me more excited. A while ago I saw Carman when he was back for a weekend, and, though I didn't write it down, I remember his address because he joked about it.

"Just think of thirteen turtles walking down the road," he said. That was it, 13 Turtlewalk Road.

Now that I have decided to go, I want to save all the time and distance I can. Two miles along the lake road, I turn east following a creek that winds through the bush. Though the path is rocky in parts and I have to watch my step, most of it is smooth and wide.

Boog runs past me and disappears into the bush up ahead. Seeing him makes me sad, because I know how hard it's going to be to leave him behind. I tried to think of some way I could take him with me, but I know that he would never be happy in the city. Then I remembered Aunt Budge once saying that if she had a dog she would want it to be like Boog. He'll be happy there, because he likes her, too.

Out of the bush and onto a dirt road that takes me to her place, I notice that something isn't right. My wind? My stride?

Before I can think anymore about it, I am there, and as I go up the lane, I see that her car is gone. Boog circles the house, barking loudly. Although I want to see her before I go, I'm relieved that she's gone to church. I know it would be hard not to let her talk me out of it. This way is sneaky, but at least I'll be gone.

Her back door is padlocked, so I look in the shed for what I need. Because there are no windows, I leave the door open and Boog comes in to sniff around. I find a piece of cardboard, but there is no rope. After watching him for a minute, I know what I have to do, although it's not what I wanted. He comes like a black ghost out of the darkness when I call. Already, as I bend to say goodbye, my throat is tight, my eyes full of tears. I say no words, but circle his neck with my arms. As if starting to know what is happening, he whimpers. I tell him to stay, then go to the door. When I turn to close it, he takes a step toward me, confused. Quickly I close and hook it, then stand for a minute listening. He knows I'm still here and waits quietly to see what game we're playing. For the first time since deciding to go, I am unsure, and for a while longer I stand. Am I really doing this – locking Boog up in a shed so I can run away? It seems wrong. But then I think about home, and it's enough to get me moving again. I dig in my pockets for the pencil stub I keep and come across what my mother gave me for Aunt Budge. It's a photograph of my parents that must have been taken just before my father died, one that I haven't seen before. They stand beside my father's car, my father looking at the camera, my mother looking at him. Aunt Budge probably took the picture. It looks as if she has just called to my father, because the camera has caught him with a look that he hardly ever had – serious, maybe even sad. My mother, too, is caught with a faint smile and a brightness in her eyes, her hand in mid-air, just above my father's arm. Suddenly, I can't look any longer. I stand, jamming the picture back into my pocket and start to print a message on the cardboard. My hand shakes, the pencil barely shows up, but it will do. Boog whimpers in the shed, then barks.

Aunt Budge, left because I have to. Can't take home any longer. Boog is yours now, I'll be with a friend – don't worry. Love, Peter.

I fold it and wedge it in beside the door handle, then, after glancing again toward the shed, I trot back down the laneway to the road, hearing Boog bark and rattle the door as he jumps against it.

The highway is good to run on, like the track at school, my feet barely seem to touch it as I go. But after a while, I start to have the feeling again that something is wrong. I have only come about four miles, and my breathing already is too hard and quick. Another mile. I concentrate on what Mr. Quinto, my track coach, teaches me: *Use you mind to beat the distance. Distract yourself from the tiredness*. I see myself in the last miles before the city, still strong and sure in my stride, still with the power. I try to bring it back, to feel it come into me now, but it won't. There is only the pain of going on. Six miles, but it feels like sixty. I go on until the highway becomes a haze. I see the photograph again: my father looking straight at me; the great love in my mother's eyes as she looks at him. Great love where there is only sadnesss now. My body burns; my feet pound as I make them go.

▲

PETER BLUE CLOUD (ARONIAWENRATE)

Weaver Spider's Web

Coyote was starving and freezing, and here it was only mid-winter. He'd forgotten to gather firewood and food. He'd planned on singing a very powerful song to make the winter a mild one, easy to live with, but he'd forgotten to sing the song.

The reason he'd forgotten was that he was fascinated by Weaver Spider who'd moved into the entrance of Coyote's roundhouse and, there, had begun to weave the most intricate web imaginable.

Now Weaver Spider knew that Coyote was watching him, and he really showed off. He'd work on a tiny section of web, turning it into miniature landscapes with mountains and plants and creatures running all around. And Coyote just sat there on his butt watching the work in progress and making up little stories to go with each picture.

Yes, Coyote thought, this is very important to watch: I am learning many things in my head.

Weaver Spider was, of course, doing all this so that Coyote would starve and die. He wanted Coyote's house so he could get married and raise a family. And so he kept weaving to hypnotize Coyote, stopping only to eat an occasional bug. Whenever a bug got stuck in his web, he would sing, "Tee-vee-vee-vee," a song which put the bug to sleep and, so, ready to eat.

"Cousin, you're looking very skinny and sick. And it's sure cold in here!" said Grey Fox when he stopped by one day. Coyote agreed, but insisted that watching Weaver Spider was very important. "I am becoming much smarter," he said.

Grey Fox watched the weaving, but being a practical person, it didn't much move him. Instead he became suspicious of the spider, convinced that he was up to no good.

Grey Fox felt pity for Coyote and went home to get food, and his axe for firewood.

Coyote ate the pine nuts and deer jerky while Grey Fox cut firewood. Then Grey Fox built a warming fire and suggested that maybe Coyote wanted to borrow the axe.

But Coyote just sat there, eating up all the food and saying, "Yes, I am becoming much smarter."

Grey Fox got fed up with this nonsense. He sang a sleep song and a dream song, and soon Coyote was snoring away.

"Now," Grey Fox said to Weaver Spider, "I know you're up to no good. I want you to pack up and leave right now; if you don't, I'm going to have you for a snack." Weaver Spider got scared and quickly left.

Grey Fox tore away the spider's web and woke Coyote up. Coyote looked at the clear sky where the web had been and saw how beautiful it all was. This new clarity, he assured his cousin, had been brought about from watching the spider. And again he said, "Yes, I am much smarter now."

Grey Fox was angry with Coyote. "I'm going to make you twice as smart!" he said. "I'm going to give you a wife, then you can have children to pass your great wisdom on to." And Grey Fox picked up his axe and cut Coyote in half, from head to asshole. Then he sang a song and brought the halves alive. The better half turned out to be Coyote Woman.

"Now you are twice as smart," said Grey Fox. And Coyote Woman looked all around, then turned to Coyote, "Why don't you go catch some mice for dinner? And while you're out there, cut some firewood, too."

And Coyote went out to do her bidding. After he'd gone, she turned to me and sort of looked me over before saying, "I suppose you think you'll be winning over women with your cute stories, huh? Well, let me tell you, you got a long way to go yet."

EMMA LEE WARRIOR

Compatriots

Lucy heard the car's motor wind down before it turned off the gravel road a quarter of a mile west of the house. Maybe it was Bunky. She hurried and left the outhouse. She couldn't run if she wanted to. It would be such a relief to have this pregnancy over with. She couldn't see the colour of the vehicle, for the slab fence was between the house and the road. That was just as well. She'd been caught in the outhouse a few times, and it still embarrassed her to have a car approach while she was in there.

She got inside the house just as the car came into view. It was her aunt, Flora. Lucy looked at the clock. It was seven-thirty. She wondered what was going on so early in the morning. Flora and a young white woman approached the house. Bob barked furiously at them. Lucy opened the door and yelled at him. "I don't know what's wrong with Bob; he never barks at me," said Flora.

"He's probably barking at her," explained Lucy. "Not many whites come here."

"Oh, this is Hilda Afflerbach. She's from Germany," began Flora. "Remember? I told you I met her at the Calgary Stampede? Well, she got off the seven o'clock bus, and I don't have time to drive her all the way down to my house. I took her over to my mother's, but she's getting ready to go to Lethbridge. Can she stay with you till I get off work?"

Lucy smiled. She knew she was boxed in. "Yeah, but I've got no running water in the house. You have to go outside to use the toilet," she said, looking at Hilda.

"Oh, that's okay," her aunt answered. "She's studying about Indians, anyway. Might as well get the true picture, right? Oh, Hilda, this is my niece, Lucy." Flora lowered her voice and asked, "Where's Bunky?"

"He never came home last night. I was hoping it was him coming home. He's not supposed to miss anymore work. I've got his lunch fixed in case he shows up." Lucy poured some water from a blue plastic water jug into a white enamel basin and washed her hands and face. "I haven't even had time to make coffee. I couldn't sleep waiting for him to come home." She poured water into a coffeemaker and measured out the coffee into the paper filter.

"I'd have some coffee if it was ready, but I think I'd better get to work. We have to punch in now; it's a new rule. Can't travel on Indian time anymore," said Flora. She opened the door and stepped out, then turned to say, "I think the lost has returned," and continued down the steps.

The squeak of the dusty truck's brakes signalled Bunky's arrival. He strode toward the door, barely acknowledging Flora's presence. He came in and took the lunch pail Lucy had. "I stayed at Herbie's," was all he said before he turned and went out. He started the truck and beeped the horn.

"I'll go see what he wants." She motioned to Flora to wait.

When Bunky left, she went to Flora: "Maybe it's a good thing you came here. Bunky didn't want to go to work 'cause he had a hangover. When he found out Hilda was going to be here all day, he decided he'd rather go to work."

"If I don't have to leave the office this afternoon, I'll bring the car over and you can drive Hilda around to look at the reserve, okay?"

"Sure, that'll be good. I can go and do my laundry in Spitzee." She surveyed the distant horizon. The Rockies were spectacular, blue and distinct. It would be a nice day for a drive. She hoped it would be a repeat of yesterday, not too hot, but, as she stood there, she noticed tiny heat waves over the wheat fields. Well, maybe it won't be a repeat, she thought. Her baby kicked inside of her, and she said, "Okay, I'd better go tend to the guest." She didn't relish having a white visitor, but Flora had done her a lot of favours and Hilda seemed nice.

And she was. Hilda made friends with the kids, Jason and Melissa, answering their many questions about Germany as Lucy cooked. She ate heartily, complimenting Lucy on her cooking even though it was only the usual scrambled eggs and fried potatoes with toast and coffee. After payday, there'd be sausages or ham, but payday was Friday and today was only Tuesday.

"Have you heard of Helmut Walking Eagle?" Hilda wanted to know.

"Yeah, well, I really don't know him to talk to him, but I know what he looks like. He's from Germany, too. I always see him at Indian dances. He dresses up like an Indian." She had an urge to tell her that most of the Indians wished Helmut would disappear.

"I want to see him," Hilda said. "I heard about him and I read a book he wrote. He seems to know a lot about the Indians, and he's been accepted into their religious society. I hope he can tell me things I can take home. People in Germany are really interested in Indians. They even have clubs."

Lucy's baby kicked, and she held her hand over the spot. "My baby kicks if I sit too long. I guess he wants to do the dishes."

Hilda got up quickly and said, "Let me do the dishes. You can take care of the laundry."

"No, you're the visitor. I can do them," Lucy countered. But Hilda was persistent, and Lucy gave in.

Flora showed up just after twelve with the information that there was a sun-dance going on on the north side of the reserve. "They're already camping. Let's go there after work. Pick me up around four."

"I can't wait to go to the sun-dance! Do you go to them often?" Hilda asked Lucy.

"No, I never have. I don't know much about them," Lucy said.

"But why? Don't you believe in it? It's your culture!" Hilda's face showed concern.

"Well, they never had sun-dances here – in my whole life there's never been a sun-dance here."

"Really, is that true? But I thought you have them every year here."

"Not here. Over on the Blood Reserve they do and some places in the States. but not here."

"But don't you want to go to a sun-dance? I think it's so exciting!" Hilda moved forward in her seat and looked hopefully at Lucy.

Lucy smiled at her eagerness. "No, I don't care to go. It's mostly those mixed-up people who are in it. You see, Indian religion just came back here on the reserve a little while ago, and there are different groups who all quarrel over which way to practise it. Some use Sioux ways, and others use Cree. It's just a big mess," she said, shaking her head.

Hilda looked at Lucy, and Lucy got the feeling she was telling her things she didn't want to hear.

Lucy had chosen this time of day to do her wash. The Happy Suds Laundromat would be empty. As a rule, the Indians didn't show up till after lunch with their endless garbage bags of laundry.

After they had deposited their laundry in the machines, Lucy, Hilda, and the kids sauntered down the main street to a cafe for lunch. An unkempt Indian man dogged them, talking in Blackfoot.

"Do you know what he's saying?" asked Hilda.

"He wants money. He's related to my husband. Don't pay any attention to him. He always does this," said Lucy. "I used to give him money, but he just drinks it up."

The cafe was a cool respite from the heat outside, and the cushioned seats in the booth felt good. They sat by the window and ordered hamburgers, fries, and lemonade. The waitress brought tall, frosted glasses, and beads of water dripped from them.

"Hello, Lucy," a man's shaky voice said, just when they were really enjoying their lunch. They turned to look at the Indian standing behind Hilda. He was definitely ill. His eyes held pain, and he looked as though he might collapse from whatever ailed him. His hands shook, perspiration covered his face, and his eyes roamed the room constantly.

Lucy moved over to make room for him, but he kept standing and asked her, "Could you give me a ride down to Badger? The cops said I have to leave town. I don't want to stay 'cause they might beat me up."

"Yeah, we're doing laundry. I've got Flora's car. This is her friend, Hilda. She's from Germany."

The sick man barely nodded at her, then, turning back to Lucy, he asked her, "Do you have enough to get me some soup. I'm really hungry."

Lucy nodded and the man said, "I'll just sit in the next booth."

"He's my uncle," Lucy explained to Hilda as she motioned to the waitress. "His name is Sonny."

"Order some clear soup or you'll get sick," Lucy suggested to her uncle.

He nodded, as he pulled some paper napkins out of a chrome container on the table and wiped his face.

The women and children left Sonny with his broth and returned to the laundromat. As they were folding the clothes, he came in. "Here, I'll take these," he said, taking the bags from Lucy. His hands shook, and the effort of lifting the bags was clearly too much for him. "That's okay," protested Lucy, attempting to take them from him, "they're not that heavy. Clothes are always lighter after they've been washed."

"Hey, Lucy, I can manage. You're not supposed to be carrying big things around in your condition." Lucy let him take the plastic bags, which he dropped several times before he got to the car. The cops had probably tired of putting him in jail and sending him out each morning. She believed the cops did beat up Indians, although none was ever brought to court over it. She'd take Sonny home, and he'd straighten out for a few weeks till he got thirsty again, and he'd disappear as soon as he got money. It was no use to hope he'd stop drinking. Sonny wouldn't quit drinking till he quit living.

As they were pulling out of town, Lucy remembered she had to get some Kool-Aid and turned the car into the Stop-n-Go Mart. Hilda got out with her and noticed the man who had followed them through the street sitting in the shade of a stack of old tires.

"Hey, tamohpomaat sikaohki," he told Lucy on her way into the store.

"What did he say? Sikaohki?" queried Hilda.

The Kool-Aid was next to the cash register and she picked up a few packages, and laid them on the counter with the money. When the cashier turned to the register, Lucy poked Hilda with her elbow and nodded her head toward the sign behind the counter. Scrawled unevenly in big, black letters, it said, "Ask for Lysol, vanilla, and shaving lotion at the counter."

They ignored the man on the way to the car. "That's what he wants; he's not allowed to go into the stores 'cause he steals it. He wanted vanilla. The Indians call it 'sikaohki'; it means 'black water.'"

Although the car didn't have air-conditioning, Lucy hurried toward it to escape the blistering heat. When she got on the highway, she asked her uncle, "Did you hear anything about a sundance?"

At first he grunted a negative "Huh-uh," then, "Oh, yeah, it's across the river, but I don't know where. George Many Robes is camping there. Saw him this morning. Are you going there?"

"Flora and Hilda are. Hilda wants to meet that German guy, Helmut Walking Eagle. You know, that guy who turned Indian?"

"Oh yeah, is he here?" he said indifferently, closing his eyes.

"Probably. He's always in the middle of Indian doings," said Lucy.

"Shit, that guy's just a phony. How could anybody turn into something else? Huh? I don't think I could turn into a white man if I tried all my life. They wouldn't let me, so how does that German think he can be an Indian. White people think they can do anything – turn into Chinese or Indian – they're crazy!"

Sonny laid his head back on the seat and didn't say another word. Lucy felt embarrassed, but she had to agree with him; it seemed that Indians had come into focus lately. She'd read in the papers how some white woman in Hollywood became a medicine woman. She was selling her book on her life as a medicine woman. Maybe some white person or other person who wasn't Indian would get fooled by that book, but not an Indian. She herself didn't practise Indian religion, but she knew enough about it to know that one didn't just join an Indian religious group if one were not raised with it. That was a lot of the conflict going on among those people who were involved in it. They used sacred practices from other tribes, Navajo and Sioux, or whatever pleased them.

The heat of the day had reached its peak, and trails of dust hung suspended in the air wherever cars or trucks travelled the gravel roads on the reserve. Sonny fashioned a shade behind the house underneath the clothesline in the deep grass, spread a blanket, and filled a gallon jar from the pump. He covered the water with some old coats, lay down, and began to sweat the booze out.

The heat waves from this morning's forecast were accurate. It was just too hot. "Lordy, it's hot," exclaimed Lucy to Hilda as they brought the laundry in. "It must be close to ninety-five or one hundred. "Let's go up to Badger to my other aunt's house. She's got a tap by her house and the kids can cool off in her sprinkler. "Come on, you kids. Do you want to go run in the sprinkler?"

The women covered the windows on the west side where the sun would shine. "I'm going to leave all the windows open to let the air in," said Lucy, as she walked around the house pushing them up.

Lucy's aunt's house sat amongst a clutter of junk. "Excuse the mess," she smiled at Hilda, waving her arm over her yard. "Don't wanna throw it away, it might come in handy." There were thick grass and weeds crisscrossed with paths to and from the clothesline, the outhouse, the woodstove. Lucy's aunt led them to an arbour shaded with huge spruce branches.

"This is nice," cooed Hilda, admiring the branches. Lucy's aunt beamed, "Yes, I told my old man, 'Henry, you get me some branches that's not gonna dry up and blow away,' and he did. He knows what's good for him. You sit down right here, and I'll get us some drinks." She disappeared and soon returned with a large thermos and some plastic tumblers.

They spent the afternoon hearing about Henry, as they watched the kids run through the sprinkler that sprayed the water back and forth. Once in a while, a suggestion of a breeze would touch the women, but it was more as if they imagined it.

Before four, they left to pick Flora up and headed back to Lucy's. "It's so hot after being in that cool cement building all day!" exclaimed Flora, as she settled herself into the car's stifling interior. "One thing for sure, I'm not going home to cook anything. Lucy, do you think Bunky would mind if you came with us? I'll get us some Kentucky Fried Chicken and stuff in town so you don't have to cook. It's too hot to cook, anyway." She rolled up a newspaper and fanned her face, which was already beginning to flush.

"No, he won't care. He'll probably want to sleep. We picked Sonny up in town. Both of them can lie around and get better. The kids would bother them if we were there."

It was a long ride across the Napi River toward the Porcupine Hills. A few miles from the Hills, they veered off until they were almost by the river. "Let's get off," said Flora.

Hilda gasped at what she saw before her. There was a circle of tepees and tents with a large open area in the middle. Exactly in the centre of the opening was a circular structure covered with branches around the sides. Next to this was a solitary unpainted tepee. Some of the tepees were painted with lines around the bottom; others had orbs bordering them, and yet others had animal figures painted on them. Smoke rose from stoves outside the tepees as people prepared their evening meals. Groups of horses stood languidly in the waning heat of the day, their heads resting on one another's backs and their tails occasionally flicking insects away. The sound of bantering children and yapping dogs carried to where they stood.

"Let's eat here," the kids said, poking their head to look in the bags of food. Flora and Lucy spread a blanket on the ground, while Hilda continued to stand where she was, surveying the encampment. Flora pointed out the central leafy structure as the sacred area of prayer and dance.

"The tepee next to it is the sacred tepee. That's where the holy woman who is putting up the sun-dance stays the entire time. That's where they have the ceremonies."

"How many sun-dances have you been to?" asked Hilda.

"This is my first time, but I know all about this from books," said Flora. "Helmut Walking Eagle wrote a book about it, too. I could try to get you one. He sells them cheaper to Indians."

Hilda didn't eat much and kept looking down at the camp. "It's really beautiful," she said, as if to herself.

"Well, you better eat something before you get left out," advised Lucy. "These kids don't know when to stop eating chicken."

"Yeah," agreed Flora. "Then we can go down and see who's all there." Hilda had something to eat, and then they got back into the car and headed down toward the encampment. They drove around the edge of the camp and stopped by Flora's cousin's tent. "Hi, Delphine," said Flora, "I didn't know you were camping here."

Lucy knew Flora and Delphine were not especially close. Their fathers were half-brothers, which made them half-cousins. Delphine had grown up Mormon and had recently turned to Indian religion, just as Flora had grown up Catholic and was now exploring traditional beliefs. The same could be said about many of the people here. To top things off, there was some bad feeling between the cousins about a man, some guy they both had been involved with in the past.

"Can anybody camp here? I've got a tepee. How about if I camp next to you."

Delphine bridled. "You're supposed to camp with your own clan."

Flora looked around the camp. "I wonder who's my clan. Say, there's George Many Robes, he's my relation on my dad's side. Maybe I'll ask him if I can camp next to him.

Delphine didn't say anything but busied herself with splitting kindling from a box of sawn wood she kept hidden underneath a piece of tarp. Jason spied a thermos under the tarp and asked for a drink of water.

"I have to haul water, and nobody pays for my gas," grumbled Delphine, as she filled a cup halfway with water.

"Oh, say," inquired Flora, "do you know if Helmut Walking Eagle is coming here? This girl is from Germany, and she wants to see him."

"Over there, that big tepee with a Winnebago beside it. That's his camp," Delphine answered, without looking at them.

"Is she mad at you?" Jason asked Flora.

"Yeah, it must be the heat," Flora told him with a little laugh.

Elsie Walking Eagle was cooking the evening meal on a camp stove outside the tepee. She had some folding chairs that Lucy would've liked to sit down in, but Elsie didn't ask any of them to sit down though she was friendly enough.

"Is your husband here?" asked Flora.

"No, he's over in the sacred tepee," answered Elsie.

"How long is he going to take?"

"Oh, he should be home pretty soon," Elsie said, tending her cooking.

"Do you mind if we just wait? I brought this girl to see him. She's from Germany, too," Flora said.

Lucy had never seen Helmut in anything other than Indian regalia. He was a smallish man with blond hair, a broad face, and a large thin nose. He wore his hair in braids and always wore round, pink shell earrings. Whenever Lucy saw him, she was reminded of the Plains Indian Museum across the line.

Helmut didn't even glance at the company but went directly inside the tepee. Flora asked Elsie, "Would you tell him we'd like to see him?"

"Just wait here. I'll go talk to him," Elsie said, and followed her husband inside. Finally, she came out and invited them in. "He doesn't have much time to talk with you, so . . ." Her voice trailed off.

The inside of the tepee was stunning. It was roomy, and the floor was covered with buffalo hides. Backrests, wall hangings, parfleche bags, and numerous artifacts were magnificently displayed. Helmut Walking Eagle sat resplendent amidst his wealth. The women were dazzled. Lucy felt herself gaping and had to shush her children from asking any questions.

Helmut looked at them intently and rested his gaze on Hilda. Hilda walked toward him, her hand extended in greeting, but Helmut ignored it. Helmut turned to his wife and asked in Blackfoot, "Who is this?"

"She says she's from Germany," was all Elsie said, before making a quick move toward the door.

"Wait!" he barked in Blackfoot, and Elsie stopped where she was.

"I only wanted to know if you're familiar with my home town Weisbaden?" said Hilda.

"Do you know what she's talking about?" Helmut asked Elsie in Blackfoot. Elsie shook her head in a shamed manner.

"Why don't you ask *her* questions about Germany?" He hurled the words at Hilda, then, looking meanly at his wife, he added, "She's been there." Elsie flinched, and, forcing a smile, waved weakly at the intruders and asked them in a kind voice to come outside. As Lucy waited to leave, she looked at Helmut whose jaw twitched with resentment. His anger seemed to be tangibly reaching out to them.

"Wow!" whispered Hilda in Lucy's ear.

Outside, Flora touched a book on the fold-out table. Its title read *Indian Medicine* and in smaller letters, *A Revival of Ancient Cures and Ceremonies*. There was a picture of Helmut and Elsie on the cover. Flora asked, "Is this for sale?"

"No, that one's for someone here at camp, but you can get them in the bookstores."

"How much are they?" Flora asked, turning the book over.

"They're twenty-seven dollars. A lot of work went into it," Elsie replied.

Helmut, in Blackfoot, called out his wife's name, and Elsie said to her unwelcome callers, "I don't have time to visit. We have a lot of things to do." She left them and went in to her husband.

"Do you think she wrote that book?" Lucy asked Flora.

"He's the brains; she's the source," Flora said. "Let's go. My kids are probably wondering what happened to me."

"I'm sorry I upset her husband. I didn't mean to," said Hilda. "I thought he would be willing to teach me something, because we're both German."

"Maybe you could buy his book," suggested Lucy.

"Look," said Flora, "if you're going to be around for a while, I'm going to a sun-dance this next weekend. I'm taking a few days off work. I have a friend up north who can teach you about Indian religion. She's a medicine woman. She's been to Germany. Maybe she even went to your home town.

"Oh, really!" gushed Hilda. "Of course, I'll be around. I'd love to go with you and meet your friends."

"You can come into the sweat with us. First, you'll need to buy four square yards of cotton . . ." began Flora.

But Hilda wasn't really listening to her. She looked as if she were already miles and miles away in the north country. Now, a sweat, she thought, would be real Indian.

▲

JORDAN WHEELER

The Seventh Wave

The sky was wet. Jerry Ducharme stared through the screen window of his pup tent and watched it fall. Raindrops splashed his nose. He could hear footsteps and talking as people walked past, but the bushes and trees hid them. They gabbed merrily as the rain fell. Jerry shook his head. He pulled lint from his navel and scratched his belly, then a stone fell on the tent. Another one hit the car. Suddenly people began running and shouting, their feet splashing through puddles. Jerry looked up. Hail.

Lynn Lake struggled with the zipper of the pup tent, her body wet with the Pacific Ocean and the coastal rain.

"Damn it Jerry, I can't get this thing open," she muttered. Jerry sat up and undid the thing. She burst in spraying water across the tent. A drop landed in his navel. Lynn fell to the floor and cuddled up to him like young kittens do, burying herself in his warm skin. Jerry pulled the sleeping bag over her shivering body. The hail stopped and it rained again. Then the rain stopped. Jerry stifled laughter.

"It's not funny," she told him, touching her tender skull. "It hurt." He couldn't hold back. Laughter burst out and hit her in the face. She buried her fist in his stomach. Jerry felt his face burn red as the jolt filled his body. He couldn't breathe. He rolled over and pulled his knees up to his chest.

"I'm sorry, did I hurt you?" Lynn asked. Jerry groaned, waiting for his breath to come back. Lynn kissed him slow and soft beneath his ear. "I'll kiss it better," she whispered. Jerry felt the air fill his lungs. Gingerly he rolled onto his back. Lynn slid down and kissed him on the belly, then she stopped and stared at a hair. Jerry stared at the ceiling. She plucked the hair and he flinched.

"Look," she said. "It's grey." Jerry grabbed it and held it up to his eyes. She passed him his glasses. Sure enough, the hair was white.

"I'll be damned," he mused.

"I think it's distinguishing," she told him. "A sign of wisdom."

"A sign of age."

"You're not that old."

There was something in the way she said "that." He was old, but not "that" old. Old like a '65 Chevy, but not a Model T. Old like a raisin not yet mouldy. Old like a turn-of-the-century barn before it falls. Old. "Don't worry, you should see how grey my dad is."

Jerry sighed. "Isn't it time for lunch?"

Canada is known for a lot of things, but not its surfing. There's Waikiki, Ulu Watu, Kuta, but in Canada, the best known surfing spot is the West Edmonton Mall. Then there's a spot three hours west of Vancouver – Long Beach. Twelve miles of sand stretching to the open sea. At one time you could camp and drive on the beach. Then the government took over, made it a national park, and called it Pacific Rim. But at Long Beach there's surf. Not a Waikiki surf, or an Ulu Watu surf, but surf. Pacific Rim surf.

Jerry had never surfed. He was an undergraduate from Brandon attending UBC. He met Lynn there. "Lynn Lake," he mused, thinking of the Manitoba town. "I have relatives there." So they talked. Then they started going out. Lynn's friend, Georgina, had a boyfriend, Mr. Muscles, who surfed. When the July long weekend happened, Lynn and Georgina decided the four of them should do something. Mr. Muscles suggested surfing and the first thing that came to Jerry's mind was the mall. He had never heard of Long Beach.

"Look at the waves," Lynn gushed. Jerry did. They'd been there ten minutes and he was already tired of sucking in his gut. She watched Georgina and Mr. Muscles, Mike, through a pair of binoculars. Jerry sipped from his beer. He was on his fifth when the sun broke. Mike and Georgina bounded up the beach. Lynn passed him a wet suit. Jerry looked at her, confused.

"You said you'd surf if the sun broke," she told him. She reached for the boards. Jerry looked up and cursed the sun. The sun smiled. Mike moved in and assumed authority. Jerry was a novice, so he should try bodysurfing first.

"Who's body do I surf on?" Jerry asked. They laughed and he decided to keep his mouth shut. He donned the wet suit and followed Mike toward the water watching the waves break toward shore. From a distance they looked safe enough, almost pretty. His feet hit the water and he leapt into the air. Ice.

"The bodysuit will keep you warm," Mike assured him. At waist level Jerry forgot what warm was. Maybe when his first layer of skin numbed up he'd be all right. Small waves hit him. Jerry was surprised at their force. He turned and faced the beach where Lynn stood with a Nikon camera. A large wave knocked him off his feet. The salt stung his eyes. He stood up and followed Mike with a waddle induced by numbness and five beers.

They started to swim. The waves were relentless. Jerry felt like a hunk of driftwood. "How much further?" he yelled. Mike pointed to where the waves were breaking.

"Past there," he said. Jerry started getting nervous. He was in the Pacific, a mass of water sixteen times the size of Canada. He might wash ashore in Okinawa. Give me mosquitoes, he thought, bullflies, something to swipe at. The sea foamed and swallowed. Salt and sand grazed his teeth. He surfaced and there was calm.

"They come in groups of seven," Mike told him.

Like dwarfs, Jerry thought, or elevens and big gulps. Sea gulls flew overhead. Ocean buzzards. A new group of seven began. Mike and Jerry bobbed and swayed like discarded pop bottles at the sea's mercy. If there were messages in the bottles, Jerry's would read five beer too many.

"Get ready," Mike yelled. Jerry copied Mike and began swimming toward shore. The water level dropped and Mike accelerated. Jerry followed. From behind, a wave caught them. Jerry felt his body rise as Mike slid down the wave's face. The wave curled with Jerry in it, tons of water crushing in on itself. It drove him face first into the sand, then twisted and fluttered him about. Ten seconds later, the sea released him. Jerry tried to stand, but his head hit the bottom. He flipped and shot up into the sun gasping for breath. His forehead was scraped from his hairline to his nose. Mike swam over.

"Some fun, eh? What happened to your forehead?"

"A shark bit me," Jerry said heading for shore, his forehead stinging with salt.

There was a lineup at the outdoor shower. Surfers and their boards stood like totems. At the front of the line, Jerry was beneath the shower. Water splashed at his scrape as Lynn plucked out sand with tweezers. A herd of giggling kids surrounded them, some threw stones at Jerry's feet.

"Must we do this here?" he asked. Lynn squinted and plucked.

"There's no running water at our campsite. How did you maim yourself like this?"

"It was a shark."

Lynn pulled back. "All done." Jerry turned and walked into the closest bush. He came out beside a Winnebago. A middle-aged couple from Burbank were playing crib. Jerry waved and walked through to the next campsite. A surfboard rammed into him. Another muscle-bound kid peered from behind.

"Sorry," the kid said, toddling off. Jerry produced a smile.

"Are you lost or something?" Jerry turned. A woman his age was sitting in a lawn chair.

"I was taking a shortcut."

"What happened to your forehead?"

Jerry saw some instinctual, motherly concern. "Shark," he said. The woman laughed.

"Would you like a beer?"

"Sure. I noticed your boyfriend there. I'm going out with a younger woman myself." He read the licence plate on her Hyundai. Idaho. The woman returned with two Coors.

"He's my son," she said, crooning. "But thanks for the compliment." Jerry nodded, then accepted the beer.

"You seem depressed," Lynn said as they sat by the fire pit. Jerry was looking up at Orion. Orion flickered back.

"You want to go golfing tomorrow?"

"That was your first try," she said, trying to soothe him. "I thought you did well."

"It was that damn shark." He breathed in the night air and let his belly hang, trying not to listen to Mike and Georgina doing naughty things in their tent. Lynn didn't seem to notice.

"You deserve another try. Once you get it, you won't believe how much fun it can be," Lynn said. "Mike says it might help if you were stoned."

"Mushrooms," Mike called from the tent, evidently finished. "I did it in Bali. You can eat them in the restaurants there. It puts you in the perfect state of mind for letting go and feeling the rhythm of the waves."

"That so," Jerry said.

"Yeah, so come on old man, give it another try."

Jerry looked at Lynn. "Anything to save our relationship."

Lynn giggled and cuddled up to him. Jerry cuddled back.

With dawn came rain that lasted until they awoke and beyond. Muscles Mike was glum. Jerry whistled as he prepared breakfast. "Isn't that a Simon and Garfunkel tune?" Georgina asked. "My mom has all their records."

"Mott The Hoople," said Jerry. "We're out of Perrier, I'm going to the store."

Jerry trotted for three-quarters of a mile and stopped short of the Pacific Rim Groceries' parking lot. He wasn't sure if he could make it over the speed bumps. He bought a pack of smokes, a case of Perrier, and returned the Deep Woods Off he bought on their way in. "I'm from Brandon," he shrugged. "It's habit." The grocer smiled. He was a young kid. Probably from UBC, too, Jerry mused.

"What happened to your forehead?" the kid asked.

"Shark," said Jerry. The kid smiled knowingly.

"If you get in trouble, the trick is to tuck and duck under."

"Tuck and duck," Jerry repeated. The kid nodded.

The sun broke and they ate mushroom omelettes without eggs. "I don't feel a thing," Jerry confessed to Lynn as they passed beneath the needly limbs of a cedar on their way to the beach. Lynn shrugged.

"Sometimes you don't get a reaction," she said.

He peered through sea drop crystals, vaguely aware that his feet were no longer planted, then rolled lazily onto his back exposing his navel to the sky. If only our eyes were on the tops of our heads, he thought, watching the small clouds. The sea lapped at his ears. His toes touched the air and he was filled with a lightness of being. He rotated his head like a panoramic camera. The trees were upside-down, but it seemed plausible. No telling why the ocean didn't fall.

"Wave!" Mike shouted.

Mushrooms, Jerry thought. He turned and treaded before an eight foot ocean, noticing how curiously huge the curl looked. Intrigued and trusting, he watched the tons of water wash toward him. Mike was swimming frantically toward shore. Give it up, Muscles, Jerry thought, it's going to catch you. Still the wave rose. The wind of the water. Then a hurricane of wet heaved and stomped on Jerry. People on the beach gasped.

It was soft as kisses went, Jerry thought, but somehow clinical. He opened his eyes and saw Mike and a crowd of people over him. "Are you all right?" Mike asked.

"Yeah," Jerry sighed. "I felt the rhythm of the wave." He got up and walked back to the ocean, the crowd yammering in his wake. "Tuck and duck," he repeated to himself. The words imprinted in the corners of his skull (mushroom murals were everywhere else), and he tucked and ducked all afternoon between lectures on the Native perspective of the "Native problem." "We're not the problem, you guys are," he expounded. Mike wanted to escape, but they were in the ocean.

"I mastered the tuck and duck," Jerry told Lynn that night as they lay on the grass staring at the moon.

"Did you ever think of the moon in terms of gender?" Jerry wondered if she had eaten another omelette. "The moon is woman. You know, the lunar cycle, our menstruation. The sun is man, commanding, garish."

"But I like the moon."

"Of course you like the moon, you're the sun."

Jerry shook his head. "Mushrooms are dangerous, especially when bodysurfing," he said and headed to bed.

Like a miracle, the sunshine persisted. Jerry and Lynn walked to the store the following morning for more eggs and beef jerky, and met up with the woman from Idaho and her surfing son.

"No more sharks?" she asked.

"Just jellyfish," Jerry answered.

The surfer snickered. They walked to the store as a group. Then in pairs on the way back. Lynn with the surfer and Jerry with Idaho. "I'm divorced and my kid's twenty. I've got all this time on my hands," she said. Jerry watched her feet.

"I'm getting my Master's."

"What's it like?" she asked, looking at Lynn. "She's awfully young."

"Like watching Bambi."

Camp Idaho came first. Jerry watched her go fondly, then turned to see Lynn watching Idaho's son go fondly. Lynn and Jerry walked back toward their camp arm in arm, then gradually separated. When they walked into lot sixty-nine, Mike and Georgina were frying oysters. Jerry dumped the eggs on the skillet. Mike added mushrooms.

"I was thinking about what you said yesterday."

"About what?" Jerry queried.

"Indians."

"Mmm."

"Don't you think all the ethnic groups should be treated equal?"

"We're not ethnic, we're aboriginal. Are we going surfing?"

"Try a raw oyster first," Georgina said. Jerry tried it, then threw up. He saw a melancholy expression on Lynn's face. They left for the beach and her melancholy persisted. Jerry searched within himself and found some of his own.

There was wind – ocean wind – moist, fresh, and fast. It pushed back his hair like it did to the trees, their branches reaching inland. The sea stood before him, waiting. Jerry felt enticed, but intimidated. The sea was big. He could get swallowed and wash up years later in Hiroshima among the crabs and sea urchins. The Souris River never had waves like this.

As Georgina and Mike frolicked in the driftwood, Lynn leaned against Jerry as he stood contemplating the Pacific. "You would have rather stayed in Vancouver, huh?"

Jerry watched the gulls fly against the wind, others dove for fish. He wondered which one was Jonathon. Then his eyes dropped to the sand where flies picked at dried kelp.

"It's a beautiful place," he said.

"Are you gonna try again? I'll go with you."

Jerry sighed, letting out his tummy a bit too much. Mike and Georgina joined them, and they walked into the surf. The waves were still huge. Jerry tucked and ducked as the others rode, but by noon, he attempted his first ride. He missed, but felt its breaking point.

"Let's go in for lunch," Lynn yelled. Jerry shook his head.

"I'm getting the hang of it, I think." Lynn turned and went for port. Jerry turned to the sea. Come on, he thought, where's that big one. He bobbed and peered over the smaller waves looking for the larger ones. When they came, he was invariably out of position. He nearly caught a five footer, but it stuck him in the sand, reopening the gash on his forehead.

He could feel his toes going numb, despite the rubber suit. The little waves peppered his face with salt, but he watched for the big ones. A new cycle began. Wave one was little. Jerry counted. Wave two, wave three. Wave four was big, Jerry tucked and ducked, then swam out to meet wave number five. It was huge. Jerry felt the rush of water being pulled into the wave giving it its volume. "Christ," he muttered, then tucked and ducked. The fringe of the wave's swirl caught him as he surfaced, but he escaped and swam to meet wave number six. Surfers on the beach took note. They cursed themselves for taking lunch. Number six came, and it was mammoth. Jerry wondered if he'd miscounted, this was the largest wave he'd seen since they arrived. He tried looking over it, but couldn't. It rose and he swallowed, then tucked and ducked. He felt the power of the wave rush past, but he was disappointed in his retreat. If there was a seventh, he would ride it.

Jerry surfaced and looked west. Twenty yards before him was a ten-foot wall of water closing in fast. The surfers on the beach guffawed and spat. They watched as Jerry turned to ride.

Jerry swam, his arms and legs flailing. Water receded beneath him and he was swallowed up by the growing wave. Jerry swam harder. The water started to rise. The wave hadn't yet curled, but it had steepened. He looked up and behind. The wave was almost on top of him. He felt his body being picked up and propelled. He was now at the wave's mercy. It swung him up its face. Jerry nearly panicked. This wave wouldn't scrape his head – it would crush it. He saw the curl out of the corner of his eye and waited for it to crush him as his arms and legs picked up tempo. The wave curled to his right. Jerry turned to his left and the wave dropped him a couple of feet down its face. He stuck out his right hand to steer himself left and quit kicking. The wave grabbed him, and he rode.

It lasted all of ten seconds, but was an exhilarating ten seconds. Jerry frolicked in the white water like a pig in mud howling at the daylight moon. Tourists clapped. He waded from the Pacific in triumph. "Hey mister," a kid yelled. "What happened to your forehead?"

"Bodysurfing," Jerry gushed.

Further up the beach he found Lynn sitting with Mike, Georgina, and the surfer kid from Idaho.

"Great ride," Mike congratulated. "Want an oyster?" Jerry shook his head.

"We're leaving after lunch," Lynn said. "Dave is coming with us." Jerry looked at the surfer kid.

"It's a drag travelling with your mom," the kid drawled.

Jerry smirked. "I bet."

They took down Mike and Georgina's tent first. Mike scrambled to gather the used condoms. Dave the surfer was gone, packing his stuff. "Mike has four tickets to REM," Lynn said, as they packed their clothes in the pup tent. "They're at the coliseum tonight."

"Who?"

"REM."

Jerry nodded, wondering who in the hell they were. His *Rolling Stone* subscription ran out years ago. They separated their sleeping bags. Lynn rolled hers up as Jerry packed his unread Beatrice Culleton novel. He'd wanted to read it over the weekend. He rolled up his green, down-filled sleeping bag slowly. It grew like the seventh wave. Jerry stopped and sat. Lynn was tying hers up when she noticed. "What is it?" she asked.

Jerry looked at his toes, then at her. "I think I'm gonna stay."

They were silent, motionless. The words became clear. "The waves got to you, huh?" She smiled. Jerry laughed.

"I think it's best," he said. She nodded. "No hard feelings?" She shook her head, then hugged him.

Running footsteps stomped into camp. "Okay dudes, I'm packed." It was Dave the surfer kid.

There was plenty of leftover beer and food. Mike and Georgina offered to leave them. "If you get bored, visit my mom. She could use the company," Dave the surfer kid told him.

"Just hope she finds you when she gets back to Van."

"Yeah," the kid laughed. They piled into the car leaving Lynn and Jerry to say goodbye. They stood silent, then it started to rain.

Lynn waved with her fingers and got into the car. Jerry crawled into the pup tent and curled up with his novel, waiting for the rain to end. He could hear the waves crush the beach.

A little later, he was sitting with Karen, Mrs. Idaho, sipping his politically correct beer in her large tent. The rain hadn't stopped. "I've been on the same path for twenty years. I want something different now," she was saying.

Jerry sniffed the ocean breeze as it spilled through the screen windows. "I want a house by the ocean."

▲

TOMSON HIGHWAY

The Rez Sisters

An excerpt from Act I

PELAJIA:
Philomena. I wanna go to Toronto.

PHILOMENA:
From offstage.

Oh, go on.

PELAJIA:
Sure as I'm sitting away up here on the roof of this old house. I kind of like it up here, though. From here, I can see half of Manitoulin Island on a clear day. I can see the chimneys, the tops of apple trees, the garbage heap behind Big Joey's dumpy little house. I can see the sea gulls circling over Marie-Adele Starblanket's white picket fence. Boats on the North Channel I wish I was on, sailing away somewhere. The mill at Espanola, a hundred miles away . . . and that's with just a bit of squinting. See? If I had binoculars, I could see the superstack in Sudbury. And if I were Superwoman, I could see the CN Tower in Toronto. Ah, but I'm just plain old Pelajia Rosella Patchnose and I'm here in plain, dusty, boring old Wasaychigan Hill . . . Wasy . . . waiting . . . waiting . . . nailing shining shingles with my trusty silver hammer on the roof of Pelajia Rosella Patchnose's little two-bedroom welfare house. Philomena. I wanna go to Toronto.

Philomena Moosetail comes up the ladder to the roof with one shingle and obviously hating it. She is very well-dressed, with a skirt, nylons, even heels, completely impractical for the roof.

PHILOMENA:
Oh, go on.

PELAJIA:
I'm tired, Philomena, tired of this place. There's days I wanna leave so bad.

PHILOMENA:
But you were born here. All your poop's on this reserve.

PELAJIA:
Oh, go on.

PHILOMENA:
You'll never leave.

PELAJIA:
Yes, I will. When I'm old.

PHILOMENA:
You're old right now.

PELAJIA:
I got a good 30 years to go . . .

PHILOMENA:
. . . and you're gonna live every one of them right here beside me . . .

PELAJIA:
. . . maybe 40 . . .

PHILOMENA:
. . . here in Wasy.

Tickles Pelajia on the breasts.

Chiga-chiga-chiga.

PELAJIA:
Yelps and slaps Philomena's hand away.

Oh, go on. It's not like it used to be.

PHILOMENA:
Oh, go on. People change, places change, time changes things. You expect to be young and gorgeous forever?

PELAJIA:
See? I told you I'm not old.

PHILOMENA:
Oh, go on. You.

PELAJIA:
"Oh, go on. You." You bug me like hell when you say that.

PHILOMENA:
You say it, too. And don't give me none of this "I don't like this place. I'm tired of it." This place is too much inside your blood. You can't get rid of it. And it can't get rid of you.

PELAJIA:
Four thirty this morning, I was woken by . . .

PHILOMENA:
Here we go again.

PELAJIA:
. . . Andrew Starblanket and his brother, Matthew. Drunk. Again. Or sounded like . . .

PHILOMENA:
Nothing better to do.

PELAJIA:
. . . fighting over some girl. Heard what sounded like a baseball bat landing on somebody's back. My lawn looks like the shits this morning.

PHILOMENA:
Well, I like it here. Myself, I'm gonna go to every bingo and I'm gonna hit every jackpot between here and Espanola and I'm gonna buy me that toilet I'm dreaming about at night . . . big and wide and very white . . .

PELAJIA:
Aw-ni-gi-naw-ee-dick.*

PHILOMENA:
I'm good at bingo.

PELAJIA:
So what! And the old stories, the old language. Almost all gone . . . was a time Nanabush and Windigo and everyone here could rattle away in Indian fast as Bingo Betty could lay her bingo chips down on a hot night.

PHILOMENA:
Pelajia Rosella Patchnose. The sun's gonna drive you crazy.

And she descends the ladder.

---

*Oh, go on. (Ojibway)

PELAJIA:

Everyone here's crazy. No jobs. Nothing to do but drink and screw each other's wives and husbands and forget about our Nanabush.

From offstage Philomena screams. She fell down the ladder.

Philomena!

As she looks over the edge of the roof.

What are you doing down there?

PHILOMENA:

What do you think? I fell.

PELAJIA:

Bring me some of them nails while you're down there.

PHILOMENA:

Whining and still from offstage, from behind the house.

You think I can race up and down this ladder? You think I got wings?

PELAJIA:

You gotta wear pants when you're doing a man's job. See? You got your skirt ripped on a nail and now you can see your thighs. People gonna think you just came from Big Joey's house.

PHILOMENA:

She comes up the ladder in a state of disarray.

Let them think what they want. That old cow Gazelle Nataways . . . always acting like she thinks she's still a spring chicken. She's got them legs of hers wrapped around Big Joey day and night . . .

PELAJIA:

Philomena. Park your tongue. My old man had to go the hundred miles to Espanola just to get a job. My boys. Gone to Toronto. Only place educated Indian boys can find decent jobs these days. And here I sit all broken-hearted.

PHILOMENA:

Paid a dime and only farted.

PELAJIA:

Look at you. You got dirt all over your backside.

Turning her attention to the road in front of her house and standing up for the first and only time.

And dirt roads! Years now that old chief's been making speeches about getting paved roads "for my people" and still we got dirt roads all over.

PHILOMENA:

Oh, go on.

PELAJIA:

When I win me that jackpot next time we play bingo in Espanola . . .

PHILOMENA:

Examining her torn skirt, her general state of disarray, and fretting over it.

Look at this! Will you look at this! Ohhh!

PELAJIA:

. . . I'm gonna put that old chief to shame and build me a nice paved road right here in front of my house. Jet black. Shiny. Make my lawn look real nice.

PHILOMENA:
My rib-cage!

PELAJIA:
And if that old chief don't wanna make paved roads for all my sisters around here . . .

PHILOMENA:
There's something rattling around inside me!

PELAJIA:
. . . I'm packing my bags and moving to Toronto.

Sits down again.

PHILOMENA:
Oh, go on.

She spies Annie Cook's approach a distance up the hill.

Why, I do believe that cloud of dust over there is Annie Cook racing down the hill, Pelajia.

PELAJIA:
Philomena. I wanna go to Toronto.

PHILOMENA:
She's walking mighty fast. Must be excited about something.

PELAJIA:
Never seen Annie Cook walk slow since the day she finally lost Eugene to Marie-Adele at the church 19 years ago. And even then she was walking a little too fast for a girl who was supposed to be broken-heart . . . *Stopping just in time and laughing* . . . heart-broken.

Annie Cook pops up the top of the ladder to the roof.

ANNIE:

All cheery and fast and perky.

Halloooo! Whatchyou doing up here?

PELAJIA:

There's room for only so much weight up here before we go crashing into my kitchen, so what do you want?

ANNIE:

Just popped up to say hi.

PELAJIA:

And see what we're doing?

ANNIE:

Well . . .

PELAJIA:

Couldn't you see what we're doing from up where you were?

ANNIE:

Confidentially, to Philomena.

Is it true Gazelle Nataways won the bingo last night?

PHILOMENA:

Annie Cook, first you say you're gonna come with me and then you don't even bother showing up. If you were sitting beside me at that bingo table last night you would have seen Gazelle Nataways win that big pot again with your own two eyes.

ANNIE:

Emily Dictionary and I went to Little Current to listen to Fritz the Katz.

PELAJIA:
What in God's name kind of a band might that be?

ANNIE:
Country rock. My favourite. Fritz the Katz is from Toronto.

PELAJIA:
Fritzy . . . ritzy . . . Philomena! Say something.

PHILOMENA:
My record player is in Espanola getting fixed.

ANNIE:
That's nice.

PHILOMENA:
Good.

ANNIE:
Is it true Gazelle Nataways plans to spend her bingo money to go to Toronto with . . . with Big Joey?

PHILOMENA:
Who wants to know? Emily Dictionary?

ANNIE:
I guess so.

PELAJIA:
That Gazelle Nataways gonna leave all her babies behind and let them starve to death?

ANNIE:
I guess so. I don't know. I'm asking you.

PELAJIA and PHILOMENA:
We don't know.

ANNIE:

I'm on my way to Marie-Adele's to pick her up.

PELAJIA:

Why? Where you gonna put her down?

Pelajia and Philomena laugh.

ANNIE:

I mean, we're going to the store together. To the post office. We're going to pick up a parcel. They say there's a parcel for me. They say it's shaped like a record. And they say it's from Sudbury. So it must be from my daughter, Ellen . . .

PELAJIA and PHILOMENA:

. . . "who lives with this white guy in Sudbury" . . .

ANNIE:

How did you know?

PHILOMENA:

Everybody knows.

ANNIE:

His name is Ray*mond*. Not *Ray*mond. But Ray*mond*. Like in Bon Bon.

Philomena tries out "bon bon" to herself.

He's French.

PELAJIA:

Oh?

ANNIE:

Garage mechanic. He fixes cars. And you know, talking about Frenchmen, that old priest is holding another bingo next week and when I win . . .

To Philomena.

Are you going?

PELAJIA:

Does a bear shit in the woods?

ANNIE:

... when I win, I'm going to Espanola and play the bingo there. Emily Dictionary says that Fire Minklater can give us a ride in her new car. She got it through Ray*mond*'s garage. The bingo in Espanola is bigger. And it's better. And I'll win. And then I'll go to Sudbury, where the bingos are even bigger and better. And then I can visit my daugher, Ellen ...

PELAJIA:

... "who lives with this white guy in Sudbury" ...

ANNIE:

... and go shopping in the record stores and go to the hotel and drink beer quietly – not noisy and crazy like here – and listen to the live bands. It will be so much fun. I hope Emily Dictionary can come with me.

ANNIE:

Yes. I'm going. I'm running out of time. I'm going to Marie-Adele's house and then we'll walk to the store together to pick up the parcel – I'm sure there'll be a letter in it, and Marie-Adele is expecting mail, too – and we'll see if Emily Dictionary is working today and we'll ask her if Fire Minklater has her new car yet so we can go to Espanola for that big pot.

She begins to descend the ladder.

PELAJIA:

Well, you don't have much to do today, do you?

ANNIE:

Well. Toodle-oo!

And she pops down the ladder and is gone.

PELAJIA:

Not bad for someone who was in such a hurry to get her parcel. She talks faster than she walks.

Noticing how dejected and abandoned Philomena looks, she holds up her hammer.

Bingo money. Top quality. $24.95.

PHILOMENA:

It's true. Bingos here in Wasy are getting smaller and smaller all the time. Especially now when the value of the dollar is getting lesser and lesser. In the old days, when Bingo Betty was still alive and walking these dirt roads, she'd come to every single bingo and she'd sit there like the Queen of Tonga, big and huge like a roast beef, smack-dab in the middle of the bingo hall. One night, I remember, she brought two young cousins from the city – two young women, dressed real fancy, like they were going to Sunday church – and Bingo Betty made them sit one on her left, with her three little bingo cards, and one on her right, with her three little ones. And Bingo Betty herself sat in the middle with 27 cards. Twenty-seven cards! Amazing.

Pelajia starts to descend the ladder, and Philomena, getting excited, steps closer and closer to the edge of the roof.

And those were the days when they still used bingo chips, not these dabbers like nowadays, and everyone came with a little margarine container full of these bingo chips. When the game began and they started calling out the numbers, Bingo Betty was all set, like a horse at the race-track in Sudbury, you could practically see the foam sizzling and bubbling between her teeth. Bingo Betty! Bingo Betty with her beady little darting eyes, sharp as needles, and her roly-poly jiggledy-piggledy arms with their stubby little claws would go: chiga-chiga-chiga-chiga-chiga-chiga arms flying across the table smooth as angel's wings chiga-chiga-chiga-chiga-chiga-chiga-woosh! Cousin on the left chiga-chiga, cousin on the right chiga, chiga-eeee!

She narrowly misses falling off the roof and cries out in terror.

PELAJIA:
Philomena!

PHILOMENA:
It's true. I've been thinking . . .

PELAJIA:
You don't say.

PHILOMENA:
It's true. The bingos here are getting kind of boring . . .

ANNIE:
That old priest is too slow and sometimes he gets the numbers all mixed up and the pot's not big enough.

PHILOMENA:
And I don't like the way he calls the numbers. *Nasally.* B 12, O 64.

ANNIE:
When Little Girl Manitowabi won last month . . .

PHILOMENA:
She won just enough to take a taxi back to Buzwah.

ANNIE:
That's all.

Both Annie and Philomena pause to give a quick sigh of yearning.

PHILOMENA:
Annie Cook, I want that big pot.

ANNIE:
We all want big pots.

PELAJIA:
Start a revolution!

PHILOMENA and ANNIE:
Yes!

ANNIE:
All us Wasy women. We'll march up the hill, burn the church hall down, scare the priest to death, and then we'll march all the way to Espanola, where the bingos are bigger and better . . .

PHILOMENA:
We'll hold big placards!

ANNIE:
They'll say: "Wasy women want bigger bingos!"

PELAJIA:
And one will say: "Annie Cook Wants Big Pot!"

PHILOMENA:
. . . and the numbers at those bingos in Espanola go faster and the pots get bigger by the week. Oh, Pelajia Patchnose, I'm getting excited just thinking about it!

ANNIE:
I'm going.

PELAJIA:
You are, are you?

PHILOMENA:
Scrambling on hands and knees to Pelajia, and coming to rest in this languorous pose, takes a moment to regain her composure and catch her breath.

And you know, to this very day, they say that on certain nights at the bingo here in Wasy, they say you can see Bingo Betty's ghost, like a mist, hovering in the air above the bingo tables, playing bingo like it's never been played before. Or since.

PELAJIA:
Amazing! She should have gone to Toronto.

S. BRUISED HEAD

An Afternoon in Bright Sunlight

Ayissomaawa . . .

The Porcupine Hills look soft and brown as we stand gazing out over sunburnt prairie grass.

"Come on, guys. Let's go for a ride," says Hank.

Hank is boss. At least he thinks he is. He is a year older than Anne and me and is the only boy in the family. We let him get away with it, sometimes.

Anne agrees with him. She always agrees with him, especially when we have nothing to do. "We'll ask Mom to make some sandwiches."

"Good idea. Tell her we're going to hunt arrowheads."

Hank decides Anne will ride Brownie, a twelve-year-old bay gelding, same age as Hank. He chooses Hoss for me. Hank says, "Hoss needs some kinks worked out, and this is as good a day as any." He chooses Buck, because Buck is his horse and Buck understands him.

Mom packs enough food to last a week, and, as we make our way back to the corral, she comes to the door and yells, "Don't go too far into the coulee, and watch out for rattlesnakes." She mangles a dish-towel. "Keep an eye open for that bear Jerry saw last week. He says he spotted it down by the old school and later saw it moving toward the hills." She shakes out the towel and waves it. "Get home before dark." She smiles. "Have a good time."

"All right," I yell. "We'll be careful."

"Don't let her worry you." Anne picks up the sack. "There are no rattlesnakes in the coulee, and you know Jerry lies a lot."

"I know Jerry lies. I'm not worried."

Hank has the horses saddled and ready to go. He takes the sack and ties it to the back of his saddle.

A wide streak of dust rises, billows out, and kind of hangs in the air. "There's Dad," says Hank. He pats Buck's neck.

Mom doesn't look too pleased. The dust mushrooms. We hear Dad's loud laughing voice, "Hello Dawlink!" Mom takes a swipe at him with her dish-towel. "I brought company," he says.

"Isn't that old Sam?" says Hank.

Mom shakes hands with Sam; her voice carries on the breeze. "Come in. I'll make you something to eat."

Everybody treats Sam with respect. I remember walking in front of him one time, and, boy, did I ever get it from Dad. I stay out of his way, now.

Hank is all excited. "There's Les!"

Les comes running. We all think Les is the greatest. Dad picks him up whenever he needs help. He trains horses for Dad. He trained Hoss, and helps out during calving season. He travels with Dad, and, sometimes, he even drives. He seems older than fourteen.

"Hey, Les," says Hank. "You can ride Hoss."

"Where you going?" Les lengthens the stirrups. "Hunting arrowheads."

Anne and I stand there listening. They ignore us. They always ignore us.

"Hey! You kids!" shouts Dad from the house. Hank shoves me and Anne up on Brownie, and we take off. We can hear Dad shouting. We reach the coulee, and Hank reins in. Les looks at him.

"Your dad was calling."

"I know."

"You guys are in trouble."

"He wants us to stay home."

"Well," says Les. "We might as well keep going now. We'll catch heck for one thing or another."

"I know, but maybe if we stay out late, he'll cool off."

"Yeah, he'll get worried," says Anne.

"Yeah, he'll just have more to get mad about," I say.

They just look at me.

We wander into the coulees, stopping every now and then to pick cactus berries. They are green and plump, the size of grapes. Their juice is sweet and sticky. They are easy to find in the short grass, and we go from patch to patch.

As we near an outcropping of rock, Anne says, "Mom said to watch out for rattlesnakes."

"Don't be silly. Everybody knows there are no rattlesnakes in these coulees. Right, Hank?"

Hank and I agree.

"Well, how about that bear Jerry saw?" says Anne.

"Jerry didn't see no bear," laughs Les.

"Are you sure?" Hank licks his lips whenever he's worried. He does it now.

"Sure I'm sure. There hasn't been a bear in these coulees for years."

"Well, a bear could have come down from the hills."

"Look," says Les, "there are no bears in the coulee."

That settles the bear question. We stay away from the rocks. Everybody knows that snakes sun themselves on rocks. None of us likes snakes, especially Hank and Anne.

Hank licks his lips. "Jerry lies a lot."

"You still worried?" says Les.

"I just remembered Dad said he saw something out here."

"I remember, too," says Anne eagerly. "It was the day before Jerry came to visit."

"It was after," I say.

"It was before," says Hank.

Anne smiles at me. "I told you," she says.

"Come to think of it," says Les, "just before we came out, we were at the pool hall in town. Your dad, Sam, and some other men were talking about seeing something out here."

"What did they see?"

"Do you know anything about Sam?"

"Yeah. He's old, and he lives by the school," says Hank.

"You're not supposed to walk in front of him," I say. "Did you know that?"

Anne wants to know more. "What about him?"

Les looks at Hank. "Do you know why he lives there?"

"No."

"He guards the coulees."

We look at Les. He looks back. He isn't smiling. His eyes sweep over us. Then he turns and carefully guides Hoss around a clump of brittle reeds down onto a dry creek bed.

"What do you mean, he guards the coulees?"

"Just that."

"Why should he guard the coulees?" Les has me curious, too.

"Oh," says Les, "there's things out here."

"What kind of things?"

"Animals . . . other things that live in the coulee."

"You've got to be kidding. Only animals live in the coulee." Hank shakes his head and laughs.

"What kind of things?" I insist.

"You don't have to know," Hank cuts in. "What did old Sam have to say?"

In a matter-of-fact tone, Les says, "He thinks a wolverine may have moved in."

"A wolverine? No kidding!" Hank's eyes light up. He moves closer to Les. "Maybe we should forget about arrowheads and go hunting."

"I don't think so."

"But, I've never seen a wolverine. It would be fun."

"We better wait until Sam figures out what to do."

"What does Sam have to do with anything?"

"Sam knows a lot. He says they're dangerous."

I break in – "That's what Emma said."

"Yeah? What did Emma have to say?"

"You're not supposed to listen to Emma," says Anne.

"Well, she says they're dangerous and evil, too."

"Forget about Emma," Hank says, licking his lips. "She's a crazy old lady. Just how dangerous are wolverines?"

"Well, you know that bear?" says Les.

"Yeah?"

"Well, wolverines hunt the hunter."

Hank looks over his shoulder. Anne and I smile.

It is hot. Horse tails switch lazily at slow-moving flies. Saddle leather squeaks. Hooves thud dully on dry grass. An occasional sharp crack echoes down the coulee.

She stands listening to the children's voices. An outcropping of rock hides her den. Inside, it is cool and dry.

Ayissomaawaawa . . . I must be careful, I waited long. Need to grow. Strong. Strong. Strong as when I was young. It was good. Our power was strong. Must be careful. Haste betrays. I must wait. Come, boy. Come alone. Do not fear. There is nothing to fear.

"Hank!" Anne yells. "Look at the chokecherries!"

Low chokecherry bushes grow halfway up to the side of the coulee. Their branches hang with thick clusters of black cherries.

"Let's pick some for Mom," I say.

Hank dismounts. "Good idea, Girlie. Here, you hold the horses."

"Why do I always have to hold the horses?"

"Because I tell you to."

I look down at him. "We can't pick berries, anyway."

"Why not?"

"We have nothing to put them in."

"We can put them in the lunch sack," says Anne.

"Good idea," says Hank. "We can tie the horses up down by those bushes."

I must wait. Cannot hurry. Wait. Not strong. Stronger must I get. Soon. Soon. So close.

The bushes are low and evenly spaced. They look as if they were planted by someone. Anne and I fill our hats and empty the berries into the sack. We begin filling our hats again, when Anne spots some raspberries growing near the outcropping of rock.

"Come on, Hank. Let's get some of them, too."

"I'm not going over there."

Anne looks at me. I shake my head.

"Just look at them!"

"Go and get them, then," says Les.

"Yeah." Hank and I agree.

"I don't know." Anne looks at the rocks.

"Noboby's stopping you," says Les.

"There might be snakes."

"Snakes won't kill you. These snakes are just ordinary snakes," says Les.

"Then you go and get them."

"I don't like raspberries."

Ayissomaawa . . . Patience. Must have patience. Soon I will have them. I must have them. Must be careful. Not move. Too soon. Wait. Time. Old woman. Now old woman. Do not frighten.

"Let's go, then. You girls wait for us here. Okay?"

"Why do we have to wait?"

Hank is real nasty. "All right. If you want to walk down, I'm not stopping you."

"I'm not going anyplace." Anne drops to the ground. "You guys can get the horses."

Hank and Les run down the coulee.

"Do you smell something funny?" says Anne.

"Yeah, it smells like sage."

"No. Sage doesn't smell like that."

"Maybe it's dry mint."

"No. Mint doesn't smell like that, either."

"Maybe it's a snake den. Snakes like rocks, you know."

"No. It isn't snakes."

"How do you know?"

"I know," says Anne. "Now quit. You're giving me a headache."

We sit there. The sun is beating down. It is quiet. Flies drone. I feel sleepy. The sun is warm on my back.

Ayissomaawa . . .

"Anne! Girlie! Get over here."

Les and Hank have the horses. They wait while we bring the sack of berries.

"Come on. Hurry up!"

"I don't feel so good, Hank," says Anne. "I have a headache."

"Me, too."

Hank and Les look at each other. "So do we."

"Maybe we should just go home."

"We can't let a stupid headache stop us from hunting for arrowheads."

Anne and me stand there, looking at Hank. Nobody says anything. Hank looks at us. "Just around the bend is where we found them last time."

"I wonder if there are any left," says Les.

"There should be plenty."

"What happened to the other ones we found?"

"Mom still has them. She takes them out every once in a while."

Ayissomaawa . . . Horses. Horses know us. Must be careful.

"Are we going to hunt arrowheads or stand around here all day?" I say.

"We're going. Now get on that horse."

Hank lifts Anne and me up on Brownie and ties the sack to his saddle. "Ready to go?"

"Yeah."

The horses walk sideways. Their ears flick back and forth. Their eyes roll, and they jerk their heads up and down. We don't go very far.

"What's that smell?"

"Smells like sage to me."

"No, it doesn't." Anne is emphatic. I agree with her.

"Well, it doesn't smell half bad. It sure is strange, though. Wonder what's causing it." Les looks around.

"What's that?" Anne points to the rocks. I try to see over her shoulder.

"Where?"

"Over there. See?"

"It's just a shadow."

"There's something there," says Anne.

The horses balk. Hoss backs into Brownie.

"Let's go see. Let's find out what it is. Come on, Hank."

Hank licks his lips. "Do you think we should?"

We look at him.

"Well, the horses don't want to go."

Les stands up in his stirrups to get a better view. A surprised look crosses his face.

"It's an old woman."

Brownie whirls. Takes off down the side of the coulee. Anne and I hold on tight. I didn't know Brownie had that much speed. As we hit the bottom of the coulee, I see two riders loom up in front of us. Brownie stumbles, and both of us fall.

"Are you hurt?" Dad sounds worried.

"No," I say, and he pulls me off Anne.

"Anne, Anne, you all right?"

Anne lies there, trying to catch her breath. I look up and see Sam.

"Anne, you all right?"

"Yeah, Dad. I'm okay." Anne lies back and starts to cry.

Before Hank and Les can slide to a stop, Dad is already yelling. "How many times have I told you not to run the horses like that?"

"We didn't do nothing." Hank points back to the rocks. "The horses . . . they just took off when they saw that old lady in the coulee."

"What are you talking about?"

"An old woman . . . in the coulee." Hank looks at Les.

"She spooked the horses," says Les.

Dad looks back and forth, eyeing each of us. He knows we wouldn't dare lie to him.

"Did you see her?"

"We didn't get a good look," says Les.

Dad looks at us and then at Sam.

"It was near those rocks," says Hank.

"Yeah, and it smelled kinda like sage," says Les.

"You kids get home right now," says Dad. He shoves me and Anne back up on Brownie. "Get going! Stay there till I get back."

We know an order when we hear one.

Too late. Must move. Always moving. He'll come. Tired. Tired. He has power. He will come. No more.

Dad stands at the mouth of the coulee holding the two horses. Sam walks into the coulee.

THOMAS KING

The One About Coyote Going West

This one is about Coyote. She was going west. Visiting her relations. That's what she said. You got to watch that one. Tricky one. Full of bad business. No, no, no, no, that one says. I'm just visiting.

Going to see Raven.

Boy, I says. That's another tricky one.

Coyote comes by my place. She wag her tail. Make them happy noises. Sit on my porch. Look around. With them teeth. With that smile. Coyote put her nose in my tea. My good tea. Get that nose out of my tea, I says.

I'm going to see my friends, she says. Tell those stories. Fix this world. Straighten it up.

Oh boy, pretty scary that, Coyote fix the world, again.

Sit down, I says. Eat some food. Hard work that fix up the world. Maybe you have a song. Maybe you have a good joke.

Sure, says Coyote. That one wink her ears. Lick her whiskers.

I tuck my feet under that chair. Got to hide my toes. Sometimes that tricky one leave her skin sit in that chair. Coyote skin. No Coyote. Sneak around. Bite them toes. Make you jump.

I been reading those books, she says.

You must be one smart Coyote, I says.

You bet, she says.

Maybe you got a good story for me, I says.

I been reading about that history, says Coyote. She tricks that nose back in my tea. All about who found us Indians.

Ho, I says. I like those old ones. Them ones are the best. You tell me your story, I says. Maybe some biscuits will visit us. Maybe some moose-meat stew come along, listen to your story.

Okay, she says and she sings her story song.

> Snow's on the ground the snakes are asleep.
> Snow's on the ground my voice is strong.
> Snow's on the ground the snakes are asleep.
> Snow's on the ground my voice is strong.

She sings like that. With that tail, wagging. With that smile. Sitting there.

Maybe I tell you the one about Eric the Lucky and the Vikings play hockey for the Old-timers, find us Indians in Newfoundland, she says.

Maybe I tell you the one about Christopher Cartier looking for something good to eat. Find us Indians in a restaurant in Montreal.

Maybe I tell you the one about Jacques Columbus come along that river, Indians waiting for him. We all wave and say, here we are, here we are.

Everyone knows those stories, I says. White man stories. Baby stories you got in your mouth.

No, no, no, no, says the Coyote. I read these ones in that old book.

Ho, I says. You are trying to bite my toes. Everyone knows who found us Indians. Eric the Lucky and that Christopher Cartier and that Jacques Columbus come along later. Those ones get lost. Float about. Walk around. Get mixed up. Ho, ho, ho, ho, those ones cry, we are lost. So we got to find them. Help them out. Feed them. Show them around.

Boy, I says. Bad mistake that one.

You are very wise, grandmother, says Coyote, bring her eyes down. Like she is sleepy. Maybe you know who discovered Indians.

Sure, I says. Everyone knows that. It was Coyote. She was the one.

Oh, grandfather, that Coyote says. Tell me that story. I love those stories about that sneaky one. I don't think I know that story, she says.

All right, I says. Pay attention.

Coyote was heading west. That's how I always start this story. There was nothing else in this world. Just Coyote. She could see all the way, too. No mountains then. No rivers then. No forests then. Pretty flat then. So she starts to make things. So she starts to fix this world.

This is exciting, says Coyote, and she takes her nose out of my tea.

Yes, I says. Just the beginning, too. Coyote got a lot of things to make.

Tell me, grandmother, says Coyote. What does the clever one make first?

Well, I says. Maybe she makes that tree grows by the river. Maybe she makes that buffalo. Maybe she makes that mountain. Maybe she makes them clouds.

Maybe she makes that beautiful rainbow, says Coyote.

No, I says. She don't make that thing. Mink makes that.

Maybe she makes that beautiful moon, says Coyote.

No, I says. She don't do that either. Otter finds that moon in a pond later on.

Maybe she makes the oceans with that blue water, says Coyote.

No, I says. Oceans are already here. She don't do any of that. The first thing Coyote makes, I tell Coyote, is a mistake.

Boy, Coyote sit up straight. Them eyes pop open. That tail stop wagging. That one swallow that smile.

Big one, too, I says. Coyote is going west thinking of things to make. That one is trying to think of everything to make at once. So she don't see that hole. So she falls in that hole. Then those thoughts bump around. They run into each other. Those ones fall out of Coyote's ears. In that hole. Ho, that Coyote cries. I have fallen into a hole. I must have made a mistake. And she did.

So, there is that hole. And there is that Coyote in that hole. And there is that big mistake in that hole with Coyote. Ho, says that mistake. You must be Coyote.

That mistake is real big and that hole is small. Not much room. I don't want to tell you what that mistake looks like. First mistake in the world. Pretty scary. Boy, I can't look. I got to close my eyes. You better close your eyes, too, I tell Coyote.

Okay, I'll do that, she says, and she puts her hands over her eyes. But she don't fool me. I can see she's peeking.

Don't peek, I says.

Okay, she says. I won't do that.

Well, you know, that Coyote thinks about the hole. And she thinks about how she's going to get out of that hole. She thinks how she's going to get that big mistake back in her head.

Say, says that mistake. What is that you're thinking about?

I'm thinking of a song, says Coyote. I'm thinking of a song to make this hole bigger.

That's a good idea, says that mistake. Let me hear your hole song.

But that's not what Coyote sings. She sings a song to make the mistake smaller. But that mistake hears her. And that mistake grabs Coyote's nose. And that one pulls off her mouth so she can't sing. And that one jumps up and down on Coyote until she is flat. Then that one leaps out of that hole, wanders around looking for things to do.

Well, Coyote is feeling pretty bad, all flat her nice fur coat full of stomp holes. So she thinks hard, and she thinks about a healing song. And she tries to sing a healing song, but her mouth is in other places. So she thinks harder and tries to sing that song through her nose. But that nose don't make any sound, just drip a lot. She tries to sing that song out her ears, but those ears don't hear anything.

So, that silly one thinks real hard and tries to sing out her butt-hole. Pssst! Pssst! That is what that butt-hole says, and right away things don't smell so good in that hole. Pssst.

Boy, Coyote thinks. Something smells.

That Coyote lies there flat and practise and practise. Pretty soon, maybe two days, maybe one year, she teach that butt-hole to sing. That song. That healing song. So that butt-hole sings that song. And Coyote begins to feel better. And Coyote don't feel so flat anymore. Pssst! Pssst! Things still smell pretty bad, but Coyote is okay.

That one look around in that hole. Find her mouth. Put that mouth back. So, she says to that butt-hole. Okay, you can stop singing now. You can stop making them smells now. But, you know, that butt-hole is liking all that singing, and so that butt-hole keeps on singing.

Stop that, says Coyote. You going to stink up the whole world. But it don't. So Coyote jumps out of that hole and runs across the prairies real fast. But that butt-hole follows her. Pssst. Pssst. Coyote jumps into a lake, but that butt-hole don't drown. It just keeps on singing.

Hey, who is doing all that singing, someone says.

Yes, and who is making that bad smell, says another voice.

It must be Coyote, says a third voice.

Yes, says a fourth voice. I believe it is Coyote.

That Coyote sit in my chair, put her nose in my tea, say, I know who that voice is. It is that big mistake playing a trick. Nothing else is made yet.

No, I says. That mistake is doing other things.

Then those voices are spirits, says Coyote.

No, I says. Them voices belong to them ducks.

Coyote stand up on my chair. Hey, she says, where did them ducks come from?

Calm down, I says. This story is going to be okay. This story is doing just fine. This story knows where it is going. Sit down. Keep your skin on.

So.

Coyote look around, and she see them for ducks. In that lake. Ho, she says. Where did you ducks come from? I didn't make you yet.

Yes, says them ducks. We were waiting around, but you didn't come. So we got tired of waiting. So we did it ourselves.

I was in a hole, says Coyote.

Psst. Psst.

What's that noise, says them ducks. What's that bad smell?

Never mind, says Coyote. Maybe you've seen something go by. Maybe you can help me find something I lost. Maybe you can help me get it back.

Those ducks swim around and talk to themselves. Was it something awful to look at? Yes, says Coyote, it certainly was. Was it something with ugly fur? Yes, says Coyote, I think it had that, too. Was it something that made a lot of noise? ask them ducks. Yes, it was pretty noisy, says Coyote. Did it smell bad, them ducks want to know. Yes, says Coyote. I guess you ducks have seen my something.

Yes, says them ducks. It is right there behind you.

So that Coyote turn around, and there is nothing there.

It's still behind you, says those ducks.

So Coyote turn around again but she don't see anything.

Psst! Psst!

Boy, says those ducks. What a noise! What a smell! They say that, too. What an ugly thing with all that fur!

Never mind, says that Coyote, again. That is not what I'm looking for. I'm looking for something else.

Maybe you're looking for Indians, says those ducks.

Well, that Coyote is real surprised because she hasn't created Indians, either. Boy, says that one, mischief is everywhere. This world is getting bent.

All right.

So Coyote and those ducks are talking, and pretty soon they hear a noise. And pretty soon there is something coming. And those ducks says, oh, oh, oh, oh. They say that like they see trouble, but it is not trouble. What comes along is a river.

Hello, says that river. Nice day. Mabye you want to take a swim. But Coyote don't want to swim, and she looks at that river and she looks at that river again. Something's not right here, she says. Where are those rocks? Where are those rapids? What did you do with them waterfalls? How come you're so straight?

And Coyote is right. That river is nice and straight and smooth without any bumps or twists. It runs both ways, too, not like a modern river.

We got to fix this, says Coyote, and she does. She puts some rocks in that river, and she fixes it so it only runs one way. She puts a couple of waterfalls in and makes a bunch of rapids where things get shallow fast.

Coyote is tired with all this work, and those ducks are tired just watching. So that Coyote sits down. So she closes her eyes. So she puts her nose in her tail. So those ducks shout, wake up, wake up! Something big is heading this way! And they are right.

Mountain comes sliding along, whistling. Real happy mountain. Nice and round. This mountain is full of grapes and other good things to eat. Apples, peaches, cherries. Howdy-do, says that polite mountain, nice day for whistling.

Coyote looks at that mountain, and that one shakes her head. Oh, no, she says, this mountain is all wrong. How come you're so nice and round. Where are those craggy peaks? Where are all them cliffs? What happened to all that snow? Boy, we got to fix this thing, too. So she does.

Grandfather, grandfather, says that Coyote, sit in my chair, put her nose in my tea. Why is that Coyote changing all those good things?

That is a real sly one, ask me that question. I look at those eyes. Grab them ears. Squeeze that nose. Hey, let go my nose, that Coyote says.

Okay, I says. Coyote still in Coyote skin. I bet you know why Coyote change that happy river. Why she change that mountain sliding along whistling.

No, says that Coyote, look around my house, lick her lips, make them baby noises.

Maybe it's because she is mean, I says.

Oh, no, says Coyote. That one is sweet and kind.

Maybe it's because that one is not too smart.

Oh, no, says Coyote. That Coyote is very wise.

Maybe it's because she made a mistake.

Oh, no, says Coyote. She made one of those already.

All right, I says. Then Coyote must be doing the right thing. She must be fixing up the world so it is perfect.

Yes, says Coyote. That must be it. What does that brilliant one do next?

Everyone knows what Coyote does next, I says. Little babies know what Coyote does next.

Oh no, says Coyote. I have never heard this story. You are a wonderful storyteller. You tell me your good Coyote story.

Boy, you got to watch that one all the time. Hide them toes.

Well, I says. Coyote thinks about that river. And she thinks about that mountain. And she thinks somebody is fooling around. So she goes looking around. She goes looking for that one who is messing up the world.

She goes to the north, and there is nothing. She goes to the south, and there is nothing there, either. She goes to the east, and there is still nothing there. She goes to the west, and there is a pile of snow tires.

And there is some televisions. And there is some vacuum cleaners. And there is a bunch of pastel sheets. And there is an air humidifier. And there is a big mistake sitting on a portable gas barbecue reading a book. Big book. Department store catalogue.

Hello, says that mistake. Maybe you want a hydraulic jack.

No, says that Coyote. I don't want one of them. But she don't tell that mistake what she wants because she don't want to miss her mouth again. But when she thinks about being flat and full of stomp holes, that butt-hole wakes up and begins to sing. Pssst. Pssst.

What's that noise? says that big mistake.

I'm looking for Indians, says that Coyote, real quick. Have you seen any?

What's that bad smell?

Never mind, says Coyote. Maybe you have some Indians around here.

I got some toaster ovens, says that mistake.

We don't need that stuff, says Coyote. You got to stop making all those things. You're going to fill up this world.

Maybe you want a computer with a colour monitor. That mistake keeps looking through that book and those things keep landing in piles all around Coyote.

Stop, stop, cries Coyote. Golf cart lands on her foot. Golf balls bounce off her head. You got to give me that book before the world gets lopsided.

These are good things, says that mistake. We need these things to make up the world. Indians are going to need this stuff.

We don't have any Indians, says Coyote.

And that mistake can see that that's right. Maybe we better make some Indians, says that mistake. So that one looks in that catalogue, but it don't have any Indians. And Coyote don't know how to do that, either. She has already made four things.

I've made four things already, she says. I got to have help.

We can help, says some voices and it is those ducks come swimming along. We can help you make Indians, says the white duck. Yes, we can do that, says the green duck. We have been thinking about this, says that blue duck. We have a plan, says the red duck.

Well, that Coyote don't know what to do. So she tells them ducks to go ahead because this story is pretty long and it's getting late and everyone wants to go home.

You still awake, I says to Coyote. You still here?

Oh yes, grandmother, says Coyote. What do those clever ducks do?

So I tell Coyote that those ducks lay some eggs. Ducks do that, you know. That white duck lay an egg, and it is blue. That red duck lay an egg, and it is green. That blue duck lay an egg, and it is red. That green duck lay an egg, and it is white.

Come on, says those ducks. We got to sing a song. We got to do a dance. So they do. Coyote and that big mistake and those four ducks dance around the eggs. So they dance and sing for a long time, and pretty soon Coyote gets hungry.

I know this dance, she says, but you got to close your eyes when you do it or nothing will happen. You got to close you eyes tight. Okay, says those ducks. We can do that. And they do. And that big mistake closes its eyes, too.

But Coyote, she don't close her eyes, and all of them start dancing again, and Coyote dances up close to that white duck, and she grabs that white duck by her neck.

When Coyote grabs that duck, that duck flaps her wings, and that big mistake hears the noise and opens them eyes. Say, says that big mistake, that's not the way the dance goes.

By golly, you're right, says Coyote, and she lets that duck go. I am getting it mixed up with another dance.

So they start to dance again. And Coyote is very hungry, and she grabs that blue duck, and she grabs his wings, too. But Coyote's stomach starts to make hungry noises, and that mistake opens them eyes and sees Coyote with the blue duck. Hey, says that mistake, you got yourself mixed up again.

That's right, says Coyote, and she drops that duck and straightens out that neck. It sure is good you're around to help me with this dance.

They all start that dance again, and, this time, Coyote grab the green duck real quick and tries to stuff it down that greedy throat, and there is nothing hanging out but them yellow duck feet. But those feet are flapping in Coyote's eyes, and she can't see where she is going, and she bumps into the big mistake and the mistake turns around to see what has happened.

Ho, says that big mistake, you can't see where you're going with them yellow duck feet flapping in your eyes, and that mistake pulls that green duck out of Coyote's throat. You could hurt yourself dancing like that.

You are one good friend, look after me like that, says Coyote.

Those ducks start to dance again, and Coyote dances with them, but that red duck says, we better dance with one eye open, so we can help Coyote with this dance. So they dance some more, and, then, those eggs begin to move around, and those eggs crack open. And if you look hard, you can see something inside those eggs.

I know, I know, says that Coyote, jump up and down on my chair, shake up my good tea. Indians come out of those eggs. I remember this story, now. Inside those eggs are the Indians Coyote's been looking for.

No, I says. You are one crazy Coyote. What comes out of those duck eggs are baby ducks. You better sit down, I says. You may fall and hurt yourself. You may spill my tea. You may fall on top of this story and make it flat.

Where are the Indians? says that Coyote. This story was about how Coyote found the Indians. Maybe the Indians are in the eggs with the baby ducks.

No, I says, nothing in those eggs but little ducks. Indians will be along in a while. Don't lose your skin.

So.

When those ducks see what has come out of the eggs, they says, boy, we didn't get that quite right. We better try that again. So they do. They lay them eggs. They dance that dance. They sing that song. Those eggs crack open and out comes some more baby ducks. They do this seven times and each time, they get more ducks.

By golly, says those four ducks. We got more ducks than we need. I guess we got to be the Indians. And so they do that. Before Coyote or that big mistake can mess things up, those four ducks turn into Indians, two women and two men. Good-looking Indians, too. They don't look at all like ducks anymore.

But those duck-Indians aren't too happy. They look at each other and they begin to cry. This is pretty disgusting, they says. All this ugly skin. All these bumpy bones. All this awful black hair. Where are our nice soft feathers? Where are our beautiful feet? What happened to our wonderful wings? It's probably all that Coyote's fault because she didn't do the dance right, and those four duck-Indians come over and stomp all over Coyote until she is flat like before. Then they leave. That big mistake leave, too. And that Coyote, she starts to think about a healing song.

Psst. Psst.

That's it, I says. It is done.

But what happens to Coyote, says Coyote. That wonderful one is still flat.

Some of these stories are flat, I says. That's what happens when you try to fix this world. This world is pretty good all by itself. Best to leave it alone. Stop messing around with it.

I better get going, says Coyote. I will tell Raven your good story. We going to fix this world for sure. We know how to do it now. We know how to do it right.

So, Coyote drinks my tea and that one leave. And I can't talk anymore because I got to watch the sky. Got to watch out for falling things that land in piles. When that Coyote's wandering around looking to fix things, nobody in this world is safe.

BETH BRANT

Turtle Gal

SueLinn's mama was an Indian. She never knew from where, only that Dolores wore a beaded bracelet, yellow, blue, and green beads woven into signs. Burnt out from alcohol and welfare, Dolores gave up one late afternoon, spoke to her daughter in a strange language, put the bracelet around her skinny girl's wrist where it flopped over her hand. She turned her face to the wall and died. November 4, 1968.

SueLinn watched her mother die. Knowing by an instinct that it was better this way. Better for Dolores; but her child mind, her nine-year-old mind, had not yet thought of the possibilities and penalties that lay in wait for little girls with no mama. She thought of her friend, James William Newton, who lived across the hall. She went and got him. He walked SueLinn back to the room where her mother lay dead.

"Lord, lord, lord, lord," the old man chanted, as he paid his respects, covering the still, warm woman with the faded red spread. His tired eyes, weeping with moisture, looked down at the child standing close to him.

"Go get your things now, little gal. Bring everything you got. Your clothes, everything."

With his help, she removed all the traces of herself from the darkening apartment. James William made a last, quick search, then told the child to say goodbye to her mama. He waited in the hall, his face wrinkled and yellow. His hand trembled as he reached into his pant's pocket for the handkerchief, neatly folded. He shook the thin, white cloth and brought it to his eyes where he wiped the cry, then blew his nose.

SueLinn stood beside the bed she and her mother had shared for as long as the girl could remember. She pulled the spread from her mother's face. She looked intensely at Dolores. Dolores' face was quieter, younger looking. Her broad nose looked somehow more delicate. Her eyes were still closed, the dark lashes like ink marks against her reddish, smooth cheek. SueLinn felt a choking move from her stomach up through her heart, her lungs, her throat and mouth. With an intake of harsh breath, she took a lock of Dolores' black hair in her small fist. She held on, squeezing hard, as if to pull some last piece of life from her mama. She let go, turned away, and closed the door behind her. James William was waiting, his arms ready to hold the girl, ready to protect.

Together they opened his door, walked into the room that was welcoming and waiting. African violets sat in a row along the windowsill, their purple, white, and blue flowers shaking from the force of the door being closed. SueLinn went to touch the fuzzy heart leaves, wondering once again what magic the old man carried in him to grow these queer, exotic plants in the middle of a tired, dirty street.

James William put aside the sack filled with SueLinn's few belongings and told the child to sit in his chair while he went to call the ambulance.

"Don't answer the door. Don't make no sounds. Sit quiet, little gal, and I be back in a wink."

SueLinn sat on James William's favourite chair, a gold brocade throne, with arms that curved into wide, high wings. She stared at the window. She looked past the violets, past the ivy hanging from a pot attached to threads dangling fresh and alive in front of the glass. She looked onto the street, the avenue that held similar apartment buildings, large and grey. Some had windows knocked out, some had windows made bright by plastic flowers. Some had windows decorated with crosses and "Jesus is my Rock" painted on from the inside. The Harbor Lights complex of the Salvation Army stood low and squat, the lights beginning to be turned on, bringing a softening sheen to the beige cement. The air was cold, the people on the street pulling their coats and jackets closer to their bodies as they walked hunched over in struggle past the Chinese restaurants, the grocery, the bars, the apartments. Cars made noises: the noises of rust, of exhaust pipes ready to fall off, the noises of horns applied with angry hands. Buses were unloading people, doors opening to expel faces and bodies of many shapes and colours. The avenue seemed to wander forever in a road of cement, tall buildings, people, machines, eventually stopping downtown, caught up in a tangle of other avenues, streets, and boulevards.

James William walked down the three flights of stairs to the pay phone in the lobby. He called the operator to report the dead woman, walked back up the three flights of stairs, his thoughts jumping and beating against his brain as his heart lurched and skipped from the climb. When he entered his room, the child turned to look at the man.

"They be here soon, child. Now we not lettin' on you here with me. We be very quiet. We let them medical peoples take care of things. We don't say one word. Ummmhmmm, we don't say a word."

He came to the window and watched for the ambulance that eventually came screaming to the curb. Two white men, their faces harried and nervous, got out of the ambulance and entered the building. A police car followed. The cops went inside the building, where the manager was arguing with the medics.

"I don't know nothing about a dead woman! Who called you? Who did you say she was?"

The officers hurried things along, the manager angrily getting out his keys.

"It's probably that Indian. She's all the time drinking and carrying on. Her and that sneaky, slant-eyed kid. Who did you say called in? Nobody let on to me."

On the third floor, cops, medics, and manager formed a phalanx around the door to 3D. Knocking and getting no answer, they unlocked the door and entered the room. Up and down the hall, doors were opened in cracks. Eyes looked out, gathering information that would be hoarded and thought about, then forgotten.

"Anybody know this woman?" the cops shouted in the hall.

Doors closed. Silence answered. One of the officers pounded on a door. A very old woman opened it, a sliver of light behind her.

"Do you know this woman in 3D? When was the last time you saw her?"

Her dark brown face resettled its lines as she spoke.

"I don't know her. I hear she was a Injun lady. One of them Injuns from out west. I don't know nothin'."

The cop waved his hand in disgust. He and his partner started down the stairs, their heavy, black shoes scratching the steps, the leather of their holsters squeaking as it rubbed against their guns.

James William stood, his ear pressed to the door panel. SueLinn continued to look past the glass. There were sounds of feet moving away, sounds of hard breathing as the body of Dolores was carried down the three flights of stairs and out into the cold November twilight.

Children were massed on the sidewalks, faces sharp and excited. Mothers called to them, the air moving with words of Chinese, English, other languages tumbling together to make one sound. Together, SueLinn and James William watched the white truck back up, turn around, and head for uptown and the morgue. The cops followed.

James William Newton was seventy years old. Singer of the blues, Prince of Georgia Blues, Sweet William, he moved from the window, went to the kitchenette, and put the kettle on to boil. He moved slowly to the icebox, then to the cupboard, taking out a pot and settling it on the hotplate. Everything surrounding James William was small and tiny like him. The table, covered in blue oilcloth, was just big enough for two. Little wood chairs were drawn tight up to the edge of the table, waiting for Sweet William's hands to arrange the seating. The one window in the kitchenette was hung with starched white curtains trimmed in royal blue rick-rack. A single wall was papered in teapots and kettles, red and blue splashed on a yellow background. The wall was faded from age but still looked cheerful and surprising. A cupboard painted white held the thick dishes and the food. Rice, red beans, spices, corn-meal, salt, honey, and sugar. A cardboard box placed on the cracked yellow linoleum held potatoes and onions, the papery skins sometimes falling to the floor, coming to rest by the broom and dustpan leaning against the teapot wall.

On the first night of SueLinn's new life, she watched James William work in the kitchen, her eyes not moving from his round body as he walked the few steps across the linoleum, taking leaves out of the tin box, placing them in a brown pot, pouring the whistling water over the tea. He replaced the lid on the pot, removed a tea cozy from a hook, and placed this over the teapot. The child, ever fascinated by Sweet William's routine, his fussy kitchen work, his hands dusting and straightening, felt comforted by the familiar activity. Often Sweet William had made supper for the girl. Cooking up the rice, a towel wrapped around his fat waist, mashing the potatoes, adding canned milk and butter. Sometimes, there were pork hocks or chitlins. The hot, pungent dishes were magic, made from the air and a little salt.

James William sang quietly as he busied himself with the pot of soup. His eyes grabbed quick looks toward the chair and the thin, gold child who watched him with blank eyes. Little folds of flesh covered her eyelids, which she rapidly opened and closed. Sitting like that, so still, her eyes blinking, blinking, she reminded the old man of a turtle he'd seen a long time ago, home in Georgia.

Poking around in the marsh, he and his friends had found a spotted turtle, upside-down, struggling to put itself right. He had picked up the turtle and looked at its head, pulling in, eye-folds closing over the eyes in panic, then opening, staring at him. He had set the turtle on its legs where it continued on. The boys had watched and laughed at the creature's slow journey. James remembered the turtle, remembered his friends, the sweetness of them. Memories like this came often in a haze. When they came to his mind, he clutched them, holding on to each minute of them, afraid never to see them again. He recalled the day. So hot and lush, you could hold the air in your hand and feel it wet on your skin. He recalled the smell of the swamp, a green smell, a salty smell. He recalled the reeds pulled from the mud, stuck between their lips. The taste of bitter grass mingling with another taste of sweet, almost like the stick of licorice his daddy had brought him from town. He tried to recall his friends, their names, the colours of brown and tan, but the memory was going. Yet, he remembered the black skin of Isaac, his best friend of all. Remembered, when Isaac held his arm, the thin fingers spread out looked like molasses spilled against his own yellowish, almost white-looking arm. Isaac?

Stirring the soup, he sang bits of song culled from memories of his mama, church, and memories of the band, Big Bill and the Brown Boys. Tunes spun from his lips. Notes and chords played in his throat, starting somewhere in his mind, trickling down through his scratchy voice-box, coming out, round, weeping, and full. Sweet William sang, his face shifting as he wove the music in and out, in and out of his body. His head moved and dipped, his shoulders shrugged and jerked to emphasize a word, a phrase. To SueLinn, it was as pleasurable to watch Sweet William sing, as it was to listen. His words and music were almost always the same. Sad and lonely words, words that came from heartache, a home with no furniture.

"Lord, what I gonna do with this here child. Now listen up, girl. You gonna be my little gal. We be mama and little gal. We be a family. Mmmmhmmm, anybody ask you, you be mine. It ain't gonna be easy. Old James William here, he gots to think of some heavy talkin' to fool them peoples be snoopin' round here. Them government types. Yes mam, James William got to think of some serious talkin'. Lord! Old man like myself with a child. A baby! I tells you, you know I never bes married. Leastwise, not no marriage like the government peoples thinks is right. Just me and Big Bill, movin' with that band. Me bein' a fool many a time over some sweet boy what talks with lots of sugar and no sense. But that Big Bill, he were some man. Always take me back, like I never did no wrong. Yes mam, I be a fool many a time. But I always got a little work. Workin' on them cars sometime. Child, I swear the metal in my blood! I can still hear that noise. Whoo, it like to kill me! That noise, them cars hurryin' along the line, waitin' for a screw here, a jab there. But I worked it! I worked it! Yes I did, and me and Big Bill, we make a home. Yes we did. We did. And before the sugar and the high bloods get him, we was a family, that fine man and me. Mmmmhmmm. Now look at her sit there with them turtle eyes. She can't talk! Now listen here baby, you mama at rest now, bless her sorry little life. You got you another kinda mama now. I take care of my baby. You mama be peaceful now. With the angels and the Indians. She make that transition over, mmhmm. She be happy. Now I gots to make this here turtle gal happy. You gots to cry sometime child. Honey lamb, you gots to cry. If you don't grieve and wail, it get all caught up in you, start to twistin' your inside so bad. Girl! It hurt not to cry. You listen to this old man. Sweet William, he know what he talkin' 'bout."

Precious Lord, take my hand
Lead me to that promise land
In that Kingdom grace is nigh
In that Kingdom way on high.

The old man began his song in a whisper. As he ladled out the soup into bowls, he switched from hymn to blues, the two fitting together like verse and chorus. He nodded his head toward the child, inviting her to sing with him. SueLinn's thin voice joined James William's fat one.

Heaven's cryin', seem like the rain keep comin' down
Heaven's cryin', seem like the rain keep comin' down
That heaven don't let up
Since my baby left this mean ol' town.

They sang together. They sang for Dolores. They sang for Big Bill. They sang for each other. Blues about being poor, being coloured, being out of pocket. Blues about home. And home was a hot, sweet, green and brown place. Home was a place where your mama was, waiting on a porch, or cooking up the greens. Home was where you were somebody. Your name was real, and the people knew your name and called you by that name. It was when you got to the city that your name became an invisible thing, next to the other names you were called, familiar names all the same. *Nigger, bitch, whore, shine, boy*. It was when you got to the city that you started to choke on your name and your breath, and a new kind of blues were sung. SueLinn often asked about home. And Sweet William sang and sang.

Precious Lord, take my hand
Lead me to that promise land
In that Kingdom grace is nigh
In that Kingdom way on high.

The man came from the kitchen and picked the child up in his arms, set her on his lap in the brocade chair, covered them with his special afghan, and the two rocked and swayed.

"She like a bird, no weight on her at all, at all. I *do* likes a rock in this old chair. It help a person to think and study on things what ails us. Yes mam, just a rockin' and a studyin' on those things."

SueLinn's tears began. She sobbed, the wails moving across the room, coming back as an echo. James William sang, crooned, wiped her eyes and his own with the dry palms of his hands.

"My baby. My turtle gal. Lord, I remember my own mama's passin'. It hurt so bad! She were a good woman, raisin' us ten kids. My daddy workin' his body to a early grave. It hurt when a mama die! Seem like they should always just go on bein' with us, bein' our mama. Yellin' to be good, bein' proud when we deserves it. You mama, she try her best. She were a sad woman. She love you, little gal. And I loves you. We be a family now. Big Bill! You hear that? A family! SueLinn Longhorse and James William Newton. Now ain't they gonna look twice at this here family? I tell you. I tell *you!* It be all right, my baby girl. It be all right."

SueLinn stopped crying as suddenly as she had started. Her thin face with its slanted eyes, small nose, and full lips subdued itself.

"But James William! I hear people talk about heaven. My mom didn't believe in it, but where will she go now? I don't know where she is! And sometimes . . . Sometimes, she said she wished I was never born."

The girl stared into the old man's face, trusting him to give her the answers. Trusting him to let her know why she ached so much, why she always felt alone and like a being who didn't belong on this earth. His skin was smooth, except for the cracks around his eyes and down his cheeks, ending at the corners of his mouth. His eyes were brown and yellow, matching the colour of his skin, like mottled corn, covered with hundreds of freckles. He had few teeth except for a startlingly white stump here and there. When he opened his mouth to sing, it looked like stars on a black map. His lips were wide and dark brown. His nose was flat, the nostrils deep.

"Baby, I don't know 'bout no heaven. My mama truly believed it. But I thinks this here story 'bout pearly gates and all is just a trick. Seem like there ain't nothin' wrong with this here earth and bein' buried in it. You mama, her body soon gonna be in that earth. The dirt gonna cover her and that be right with her. She miss the sky and the wind and the land. Told me plenty a time. Seem like, compared to that heaven where the peoples hang playing harps and talkin' sweet, this here earth ain't so bad. You mama, she be mighty unhappy in a place where they ain't no party or good lovin' goin' on! Seem like that heaven-talk is just a way to get the peoples satisfied with the misery they has to bear in this here world. Once you gets to thinkin' that a reward waitin' on you for bein' poor and coloured, why it just beat you down more. You don't gets to think about doin' somethin' about it right here, right now. Mmmmhmmm, them white peoples, they thinks of everything. But there be a lot they don't know. Everything don't always mean *every thing!* I do believe Dolores be more at rest in the brown dirt. And lord, child, from jump every mama wish her children never be born sometime! That's a fact. Mmmmhmmm. Honey, she love you. She just too full a pain to remember to *tell* you. It just like me and Big Bill. Why, they be days go by we forgets to say, Big Bill you my onliest one. James William, you sure one fine man. Then you gets to thinkin', hey, this man don't love me no more! And you gets afraid to ask, because you thinkin' that's *his* duty to remember. Then you gets mad and sad all together, and then you speakin' in shortness and evil kinda ways. You forgets that everybody be carryin' his own pain and bad things. The disrememberin' be a thing that happen though. We be foolish, us peoples. Ain't no way gettin' round that! Seem like, if we be perfect, we be white peoples up there in that heaven they thinks so special! Yes, yes, we be in that white heaven, with the white pearly gates and the white robes and the white slippers. Child! Lord child! Whooo!"

And he laughed and laughed, hugging SueLinn tight, his chest rumbling in her ear. She laughed, too, even though she wasn't sure she knew the joke. But it made her feel better, to be sitting in Sweet William's lap, her head pressed to his heart, the afghan of bright colours covering her coldness and fright. She had laughed with Dolores. Mostly over Dolores' mimicry of the people in the street or in the bars. She almost became those people, so good was she at capturing a gesture, a voice, a way of holding her body. There was no meanness in the foolery; just fun, just a laugh, a present for SueLinn.

"Now my turtle gal, this old coloured man be talkin' more than his due. I says, after a song and a good cry, they ain't nothin' better than hot soup and peppermint tea. I thinks I even gots a little banana cake saved for you."

They unfolded from the brocade chair and went to the table. The tiny Black man with his light skin. The tiny girl of gold skin and Indian hair, her body wrapped in the afghan crocheted by Sweet William's hands. The colours moved across her back, the ends trailing on the floor. As Sweet William poured the tea, his white shirt dazzled the girl's eyes. She watched his short legs walk slowly to the stove, his small feet wearing the felt slippers he never seemed to take off. He was wearing his favourite pants, grey flannel with handsome pleats in the font and small cuffs at the bottom. And his favourite belt, a wide alligator strip weaving in and out of the grey wool belt loops. The buckle was of solid silver, round and etched with the words *Florida Everglades*. It had been a gift from Big Bill, so many years ago the date and reason for the gift were lost in James William's memory. He only remembered Big Bill's face as he handed the belt to Sweet William. The dark beige of his skin flushing and reddening as he pushed the tissue-wrapped gift toward James William, saying, "Here honey. For you. A gift."

James William's starched white shirt had cuffs turned back, fastened with silver-coloured links, a red stone gleaming in the centre of each piece of metal. She looked at the stones that seemed to signal on-off-stop – red means stop.

She had learned that in school when she had started kindergarten. That was four years ago. She was in third grade now, a big girl. She liked school. At least, she liked it when she went. When her mom remembered to send her. When SueLinn remembered to wash out her T-shirt so she could be clean. When she felt safe to ask Dolores to braid her long hair without making the woman cry. When Dolores was in a good mood from having extra money and bought SueLinn plaid dresses and white socks and shoes that were shiny and had buckles instead of laces. Dolores talked loud at these times, talked about how her baby was just as good as anybody, and, anyway, she was the prettiest kid in school by far. SueLinn had a hard time understanding this talk. Everybody in school wore old clothes and shoes with laces. It didn't make sense. Maybe it had to do with the picture magazines that showed up around the apartment. The people on the shiny pages were always white and stood in funny poses. They wore fancy clothes and coats made from animals. They looked as if they were playing statues, which SueLinn had played once with the kids at school. It was a scary feeling to stop and stand so still until the boss kid said you could move. She liked it though. It made her feel invisible. If she were really a statue, she'd be made out of stone or wood, something hard. Sort of like the statues at the place her teacher, Miss Terrell, had taken them. Miss Terrell had called the giant building a museum and called the statues sculptures. She had pointed out the one made by a coloured man. She took them to the Chinese room. The Chinese kids had stood around self-consciously, denying any link to a people who wrote on silk and make bowls of green, so thin and fine one could see through to the other side. She took them to see a display case that had Indian jewellery resting on pieces of wood, only Miss Terrell had called it Native American art. The Indian kids had smirked and poked each other and hung back shyly as they all looked at the beadwork and silverwork so fantastic no human could have been remotely connected to the wearing of it. SueLinn had remembered her mother's beaded bracelet and stared at the glass case. It made her want to cry for a reason she couldn't begin to think about. She remembered the Chinese room and the Indian case for a long time after that. She told her mom about them. Dolores said it would be nice to go there, she had gone there once, she thought. But they never talked about it again. SueLinn was not a statue, but bony and covered with soft gold skin and coarse black hair that reached beyond her shoulder blades. She practised statues at home, standing on the worn, green couch, trying to see herself in the wavy mirror on the opposite wall.

"Getting stuck on yourself, honey? That's how I started. A grain of salt. That's what we should take ourselves with. We're just bones and skin, honey. Bones and skin."

The child thought her mother much more than bones and skin and salt. She thought Dolores was beautiful and was proud to walk with her on the avenue. The day they got the food stamps was one of the best days. Dolores was sober on those days. She sat at the card table, making lists and menus. Dolores laboured hard on those days. Looking through her magazines, cutting out recipes for "tasty, nutritional meals within your budget." SueLinn stayed close to her mother on those days, fascinated by Dolores' activity.

"How would you like chicken vegetable casserole on Monday? Then on Tuesday we could have Hawaiian chicken. I found a recipe for peanut butter cookies. It says that peanut butter is a good source of protein. Would you like Dolores to make you cookies, baby? Maybe we could make them together." SueLinn shook her head yes and stood even closer to her mother. Shiny paper with bright colours of food lay emblazoned on the table. SueLinn was caught by Dolores' words. Her magic-talk of casseroles and cookies. Writing down words that came back as food. Food was something real, yet mysterious. Food was something there never was enough of. And she knew there were people in the world who always had enough to eat, who could even choose the food they ate. People who went into stores and restaurants and read the labels and the columns and maybe glanced at prices, but often paid no attention to such details. SueLinn didn't know how she knew this was so, but she knew all the same. She ate a free lunch at school. Always hungry, eating too fast, not remembering what she ate, just eating, then being hungry again. Miss Terrell asked each morning if anyone had forgotten to eat breakfast, because she just happened to bring orange juice and graham crackers from home. There was always

enough for everyone. Miss Terrell was a magic teacher. Her whole being was magic. Her skin was darker than any coloured person SueLinn had ever known. Almost a pure black, like the stone set in the school door, proclaiming when it was built (1910) and whose name it was built to honour (Jeremy Comstock). Marble, yes, that's what Miss Terrell called it. Black marble, that was Miss Terrell's skin. Her hair was cut close to her head. It curled tight against her scalp. James William's hair was like this, but somehow not so tightly curled and his hair was white, while Miss Terrell's was as black as her skin. She wore red lipstick, sometimes a purple colour to match her dress with the white-and-pink dots on the sash. Her clothes were a marvel to see. Blue skirts and red jackets. Green dresses with gold buttons. Her shoes, a red or black shining material with pointy, pointy toes and little wood heels. Miss Terrell was tall and big. Some of the boys whispered and laughed about Miss Terrell's "boobs." SueLinn saw nothing to laugh at, only knowing that boys giggled about sex things. She thought Miss Terrell's chest was very beautiful. It stuck out far and looked proud in a way. When she had mentioned this to James William, he had said, "Child, that Alveeta Terrell be a regular proud woman. Why wouldn't her chest be as proud as the rest of her? She mighty good-lookin' and one smart lady. You know you just as lucky as can be to have proud Alveeta Terrell be your teacher!"

One time, and it was the best time, Miss Terrell had come to school in a yellow dress over which she wore a length of material made from multi-coloured threads of green, red, purple, yellow, and black. She had called it Kente cloth and told the class it had been woven in Africa and the people, even the men, wore it every day. She said she was wearing this special cloth because it was a special day. It was a day that Black people celebrated being African, and, even though they might live in all kinds of places, they had still come from Africa at one time. Then she had shown them a map of Africa, then traced lines running from that continent to America, to the West Indies, to South America, to just about everywhere. Amos asked if Africa was so good, why did the people leave? Miss Terrell said the people didn't leave because they wanted to, but because these other people, Spanish, British, American,

French, had wanted slaves to work on their land and make things grow for them so they could get rich. And these same people had killed Indians and stolen land, had lied and cheated to get more land from the people who were the original owners. And these same people, these white people, needed labour that didn't cost anything so they could get richer and richer. They had captured Black people as if they were herds of animals and put them in chains and imported them to countries where their labour was needed. The children pondered on this for minutes, before raising their hands and asking questions. The whole school day was like that, the kids questioning and pondering, Miss Terrell answering in her clear, sure voice. It seemed as though she knew everything. She told them about Denmark Vesey, Nat Turner, Chrispus Attucks, whose last name meant deer, because his mama was a Choctaw Indian. She told them about Touissant L'Overture, about the Maroons in Jamaica, she told them about the Seminoles and Africans in Florida creating an army to fight the U.S. soldiers and how they won the fight. SueLinn's mind was so filled with these wondrous facts, she even dreamed about them last night. And it came to her that Miss Terrell was a food-giver. Her thoughts and facts were like the graham crackers she laid out on her desk each morning. They were free to take; to eat right at that moment or to save up for when one got real hungry. SueLinn copied down her realization in the little notebook she carried with her everywhere. "Miss Terrell is a food-giver." She told James William, who agreed.

Food-stamp day. Dolores making something out of nothing. What did it mean? Everything meant something. This she had learned on her own; from the streets, from the people who surrounded her, from being a kid. SueLinn wanted to ask Dolores about it, but was too shy.

Dolores was ready. SueLinn puttered at the card table, stalling for time, prolonging the intimacy with her mother. SueLinn was not ready for the store. It happened every time. Dolores got sad. The store defeated her. It was a battle to see how far down the aisles she could get before giving up. The limp vegetables, the greenish brown meat, the lack of anything resembling the good food in the magazines. SueLinn sensed it before it came. The faint shrug of

Dolores' shoulders, the shake of her head as if clearing it from a fog or a dream. Then they proceeded fast, Dolores grabbing at things that were cheap and filling, if only for a few hours. The little girl tried calling her mama's attention to funny people in the store or some fancy-packaged box of air and starch. Anything, please, please, *that would take that look off Dolores' face. That look of fury and contempt. That look of losing. They would end up coming home with a few things like bread and canned corn and maybe hamburger sometimes, cereal in a box and a bottle of milk. Dolores would put the pitiful groceries away, go out and not return until the next day.*

Dolores picked up her lists and stamps, placed them in her purse, a beige plastic bag with her initials stamped in gold lettering. D.L. Dolores Longhorse. She went to the wavy mirror and with her little finger applied blue eyeshadow because, "You never know who we'll meet." She brushed her black hair until it crackled with sparks and life across her wide back. Dressed in blue jeans too tight, a pink sweater frayed and unravelling at the bottom, her gold-tone earrings swinging and dancing, she defied anyone or anything to say she didn't exist. "Let's go."

Her daughter took hold of her mother's hand and stared up at Dolores, as if to burn the image of her mama into her brain, to keep the smell of lily-of-the-valley cologne in her nose. The brown eyes ringed in blue looked down at her child. Dark eye watched dark eye. Two females locked in an embrace of colour, blood, and bewildering love. Dolores broke the intensity of the moment, cast her eyes around the apartment, committing to memory what she had come home to, tightening her hold on SueLinn's hand, and said, once again, "Let's go." She set the lock, and the two went out onto the street.

SueLinn's eyes closed with this last memory. Her head nodded above the soup. James William rose from the table and pulled the bed down from the wall. Straightening the covers and fluffing the pillows, he made it ready for the child's tired body. He picked her up and carried her the few feet to the bed. Taking off her shoes, he gently placed the girl under the blankets and tucked the pillow under her head. He placed the afghan at the foot of the bed, folded and neat.

James William Newton went to his chair and sat in the night-time light. He could see a piece of the moon through a crack between the two buildings across the street.

"Ol' moon, what you think? I got this here child now. Them government peoples be wantin' to know where this child be. Or is they? Seem like the whereabouts of a little gal ain't gonna concern too many of them. Now I ain't worryin' 'bout raisin' this here turtle gal. It one of them things I be prepared to do. Moon, we gots to have a plan. I an old man. This here baby needs me, yes she does. There gots to be some providin' to do. Big Bill? Is you laughin' at me? It be a fix we in. Mmmmhmmm, a regular fix. Big Bill? I needs a little of them words you always so ready with. Honey, it ever be a wonder how a man could talk so much and *still* make sense like you done! I sittin' here waitin' on you. Yes sir, I sittin' and waitin' on you."

He sat through the night, refilling his cup many times. His memories came and went like the peppermint tea he drank. Sometime before dawn, he drank his last cup, rinsed it and set it upside-down in the sink. He settled his body on the blue davenport, the afghan pulled up to his shoulders. He looked one more time at the child, her dark hair half hiding her face in sleep.

"Child, sleep on and dream. Sweet William, he here. You be all right. Yes mam, you be all right."

He closed his eyes and slept.

▲

BRUCE KING

Hookto
The Evil Entity

In the same time span as Leon was wrapping up his song, winding down to the last "... into heaven anymore," and Tanlu was blending into a cool Oklahoma night - something stirred. As J.B. caught his breath and checked his courage, Coyote was slipping down the last ridge before a gentle descent into Albuquerque. His sonar tuned to an ancient song, J.B. was hoping to hear police sirens signalling safety.

Something else was listening though the sound had echoed past. Hookto cocked his ears, straining to decipher the sound from all the other howls, cackles, and screechings his world entailed. Hookto, the changing thing, had been sleeping, too. Unlike Coyote, he awoke to sounds, incantations beseeching his presence. He did the bidding of witches and responded to the smells of tobacco powered by prayer. When Hookto slept it was usually after he'd fed. He'd been sleeping, but not for two hundred years. Now he tried to place where he'd heard that sound. When? Not recently, he was sure of that. He knew that sound and the memory of it was unsettling.

Hookto was an ancient entity, coexisting with emigrant demons and goblins that followed the light-skinned ones across the great waters. He was a member of the smoke clan, his powers being brought forth through fire and tobacco, formulated by evil incantations passed from one evil to another, a manifestation of the darker nature. He thoroughly enjoyed his existence in the darker plane. All the other demons and incubuses kept their imported asses the hell out of his way. They were afraid of him. Unlike the races of people that occupied the land of the lighter plane, Hookto and others like him had not relinquished. They frightened the new entities and kept their numbers small through rigid enforcement. They killed whatever they happened on. If it moved, it died.

Before the time of the new entities, Hookto had been engaged in a centuries-old running battle with the forces of good, the natures and laws of good, and good medicine people, and good prophets, good messiahs and all that stupid, goody goody crap that kept him from feeding. He sniffed the air briefly, hoping to catch a scent of the sound. All of Hookto's senses were interchangeable, as was his shape and imagery. Only his purpose and appetite remain perpetual.

His purpose was to feed. Ahhh yes, to feed. Hookto did not sit down to dinner to eat, he haunted. Yes, he fed by reaching within a living entity, be it evil or human, and drawing out the life force, the spirit, and absorbing that energy. It was a horrible transaction. The spirit of anything living will resist, so Hookto takes all the time he needs, twisting, pulling, shredding, letting go only to pull again, a spiritual torturer. The body may die but the struggle sometimes took days. The spirit would weaken and Hookto grew strong, excited, and when the absorption was complete, he'd sleep. He'd do this constantly, to whomever he happened upon, and once every millennium, he'd pay tribute to the Punisher and hand the ingested souls over. Then he'd start all over. This was all he'd ever known.

When he'd started feeding on the light-skinned ones, he was surprised by their immediate surrender. They'd call him Satan when he appeared to them, they flushed and shocked so much easier, holding up their silly symbolic cross and praying to an alien God, and he'd strike them down. He could smell and hear their fear when he whispered, "Yes. I am the one you call Satan, Lucifer, the Antichrist, and the fallen angel," not knowing who he was talking about but loving the fright it registered just the same. It didn't matter, light-skinned ones, the darker original inhabitants, the blacks with their exotic medicines, the island people with their own special brand of evils, he could take them all. He'd take them because they were stupid, because they were people and he fed on people, but mostly because they'd ask for it . . . literally. They wanted something. Wealth, fame, power, love, something incredibly secondary, and they'd seek his assistance.

Mostly the original inhabitants knew the incantations and his special song. He'd come to them first as someone they trusted, a gentle old man or woman, a handsome male figure, a beautiful, seductive woman. They'd invite him in and that was that. They'd know a momentary gesture of their wish and he'd let them enjoy that while he prepared to feed. When he was ready, he'd appear as their worst fear. He enjoyed the look on their faces when it would register. They were lunch, they were losers, they had stepped mightily into the ever eternal big deep and the tour guide to hell was standing in front of them with the ticket. Not many people can comprehend what it means to give up your soul, but at the moment of collection, those who dealt with Hookto knew. They pleaded and tried to redeal. They'd cry and beg. They'd try to call on the Creator, God, anybody who might matter, but once dealt with, it was over. Sometimes he'd toy with them. "Well, if you want out, you have to give me someone else," he'd tell them. They'd bring him life's rejects, old drunks, prostitutes, mental cases, other people's children, and when they got desperate, they'd hand up their own children.

To say that Hookto was without feelings would be unfair. He felt excitement, an almost sexual satisfaction when he'd feed on children. Their life force was of the purest essence, a succulent experience that offered no resistance and put him in good favour with the Punisher. He'd feed on the child immediately, right there in front of whatever parent had conceded and make them watch. They'd see the colour changes, the surges of energy as he clung to the small, frail living thing and attached himself by the mouth of his face and the mouths on the insides of his hands. He'd draw deep and inhale, ingesting the colour out of the child, and like a vampire that would suck the blood of its victim, Hookto could enjoy a black-hearted, evil orgasm that left him spent and satisfied. Instead of smoking the customary cigarette, he'd turn and feed on whoever happened to have witnessed the death of their child. He hated them because they had given up a part of themselves to save their own sickening hides when it made no difference. Like it's been said, he eventually feeds on whoever, and whatever he happens upon.

On everyone but the good ones. The dreaded good ones. There were always the good ones. They were the ones who had turned their hearts and souls over to the Creator long before he'd happen upon them. The good ones, they were the ones that his victims sometimes went running to when things had gotten out of control. The good ones were the courageous ones. They knew how to stand up to him, how to chase him away, and how to stop him. Some even had the knowledge and the means to destroy him. Not many, but enough to keep him worried and guessing. At one time, before the invasion, there had been numerous good ones, enough to keep him discreet, careful, and on the run.

Nowadays, their numbers had decreased drastically. The good ones were thinning out, getting old, becoming isolated, and there were no good ones turning out to take their place. The good ones were weakening and Hookto was celebrating by helping the process along. No one wanted to be a good one. It was too much work and commitment, too much diligence, too much responsibility. So the aging good ones were humoured, tolerated, and ignored. Sometimes they'd disappear and die and no one would miss them. Sometimes Hookto got there before natural death came knocking. He was always looking for good ones to destroy. He couldn't feed on the good ones. He couldn't ingest them. They weren't meant to be his, so he'd kill them. He'd make sure their last moments in this life were filled with terror. He couldn't come right after them. They still had power. But he'd found a way to get them to invite him in. He'd pose as young men or women inquiring to become good ones. It worked every time. Being a good one did not make you invulnerable to loneliness or adoration. He'd try to make them sin by getting them to sleep with his transformed imagery. If they did, he'd feed because they were no longer pure. If not, he'd change in front of them, from woman to man, hand to claw to hoof. He'd beat them and bite them, claw and rip them. He'd rape them, men and women, changing from owl to pig, donkey to snake, deer to bear while doing so. He'd cackle and screech, hiss and growl while he'd rip them internally. He broke their bones and he drove and ground into them. Hookto could not physically ejaculate, so he'd just enter into a manic killing, raping frenzy that lasted as long as the aging good one stayed alive. Sometimes they went insane before they died. Sometimes they willed themselves over right away, leaving Hookto to rape and rip a dead body. But none of them ever exhibited what he needed to make it satisfying . . . fear. That was the good ones for you, too damn stupid to be afraid. But in the black vestiges of his heart he knew they had won anyway. All he'd done was release them. At least he was rid of them and they threatened him no more.

Hookto was a powerful force to be reckoned with and wherever he showed there was terror and suffering. But he was not as frightening and powerful as he liked to think. He had always underestimated the power and the numbers of the good ones. He still kept a relatively low profile though he felt strong, impudent, and brazen. True, he was killing the old good ones recently, but what he didn't realize was that most of them were prepared to go anyway, and when he killed without feeding, he lost. He lost power, he lost souls he had accumulated, and he lost face, very bad for someone in the service of the Punisher.

At the moment he wasn't worried about all that. All he could focus on was the lingering howl. That sound had rippled through the darker world causing the slithering hissing things to perk up and take notice. Hardly ever did a sound from the lighter plane penetrate the darker world. When it did, every scaly, furry, horned evil thing listened. Some of the imported entities had never experienced a sound coming through their world. Hookto knew that there exists mystical monkey wrenches that do not fall within the parameters of what he, and we, believe the unseen powers to be.

Smoke is one of the accepted transcending forces that moves from the lighter plane to the darker. It usually carries with it a prayer and is said to be the strongest potion for achieving an audience with the Creator, or stirring the interest of things like Hookto. It depends on the wishes of the chanter, or the will of the one praying. One would think, or wish to believe, that good begets good and evil, suffice to say that those who call upon these darker powers, very well deserve what they get. Smoke is the acceptable whispering though, but a howl? Not hardly. If you asked someone from the lighter plane how to send noises to the other side, we'd get a glimpse of the ever-present question mark that causes spiritual leaders, priests, and holy men to shake their heads and gaze back at you like you had the answer. Coyote's howl had that kind of impact on those that roam over there. It lingered disturbingly and made them wonder if they'd heard it at all. "What was that? Did you hear it? What? Hmmm, it was probably nothing. Yeah. C'mon, let's sneak over to the lighter plane and scare some humanoid whitehead."

Hookto started moving and when he did, everything else stopped. None of the things from the other side wanted Hookto to see them. If he did, he usually zeroed in and destroyed it. Whatever the hapless thing tried to do, fly, slither, run, burrow, it made no difference because Hookto could change and follow. He could fly, run, vanish and reappear. Now, he wasn't interested in swatting insignificant things into mushed matter. He was on his way to the lighter plane. He thought for a moment about what form he should take and as he transcended through the opening, he ran as a black horse. He enjoyed both worlds and sometimes he wished he could live in both. His time in the lighter plane was restricted, five days at the best length. So as long as he existed he'd been bouncing back and forth, here to feed, there to rejuvenate, here to feed, there to sleep, here to feed, there to pay tribute to the Punisher, and so on. He had no sense of when it all began and where it would all end. He just was, and sometimes that's the best way to look at things.

For now, the horse galloped freely. A strong pace leaving a dust trail that, like the red glowing eyes, could not be seen in the night.

"Hookto" is an excerpt from an untitled novel in progress.

▲

JEANETTE C. ARMSTRONG

This Is a Story

It came to me one morning early, when the morning star was up shining so big and bright, the way she does in the summers. It was during the women's gathering at Owl Rock. It was the same year that the Red Star came so close to the earth that it was mentioned in the papers.

I had been sitting up with the fire. One woman had to sit up with it at all times during the gathering. One friend had stayed up with me to help keep me awake. It had been cold and I was wrapped up in a Pendleton blanket. It was the second to last night of the gathering. I was getting very sleepy when George said, "Tell me a story."

"Okay," I said. "This story happened a long time ago. It's real."

Kyoti was coming up the river, from the great Columbia River up to the Okanagan River. Kyoti had come up through there before. One time before that I know of. That time Kyoti came up the Okanagan River which runs into the Columbia River. That was the time when Kyoti brought salmon to the Okanagan. Everywhere Kyoti stopped at the Peoples' villages, salmon was left. It made everyone happy. It was a great gift. Kyoti did that a long time ago.

Now, after waking up from an unusually short nap, Kyoti was walking along upstream, wanting to visit with the People in the Okanagan. These were Kyoti's favourite people. Visiting them always meant a real feast with salmon. Kyoti was partial to salmon.

While walking along, Kyoti noticed a lot of new things. A lot of things changed since that last trip through here. There sure were a lot of Swallow people, and they had houses everywhere, but Kyoti couldn't find any People, or even the villages of the People. Things looked very strange.

Eventually, Kyoti came to a huge thing across the river at Grand Coulee. It was so high it stretched all the way across the water and blocked it off. Kyoti stopped and looked at it for a while not having any idea what it might be. It didn't look good, whatever it was. Something was worrisome about it. Kyoti had thought of going up to the Kettle Falls to where the Salmon Chief stayed, but there didn't seem to be any way salmon could get past that thing, no matter how high they jumped. Kyoti was pretty hungry by then, not having seen any People. Just to make sure, Kyoti decided to go up the Okanagan River to where the People had been real happy to get the salmon brought to them.

It was a good thing Kyoti didn't go up to Kettle Falls anyway. Kyoti didn't know, yet, that all the People had moved away when the Falls had disappeared under the new lake behind Grand Coulee.

So Kyoti went back down the river and started up the Okanagan. Kyoti kept going along the river and, sure enough, what Kyoti was afraid of came true. There was another one of those things right there at Chief Joseph. But this time there were a couple of People fishing there. They were the first People Kyoti had seen anywhere along the river. They were directly below that huge thing that stretched way up and across the river.

So Kyoti went up to them and waited for a greeting and some show of respect. Like an invite to eat. After all Kyoti was respected in these parts. Kyoti had brought the salmon to these People.

Kyoti waited for a while but neither of the young men said anything. They just kept on fishing. Kyoti got tired waiting for them to speak first and said, "How is the fishing?"

They both just looked at Kyoti, like they didn't understand.

Kyoti again spoke, slower and louder this time, "Is the fishing good? I bet there are some big ones this time of year."

One of them shrugged and tried to say in Swallow talk that they didn't know the language.

That was how Kyoti found out that they couldn't understand the language of the Okanagan People!

Kyoti couldn't figure that one out, but since Kyoti knew all the languages, Kyoti talked to them in Swallow talk. Kyoti asked them again how the fishing was.

They looked at Kyoti and one of them answered, "We been here two days, nothing yet."

Well Kyoti was pretty disappointed. Kyoti was hoping to eat a couple of salmon for lunch. Kyoti thought that maybe it wasn't a lost cause after all. People in their village might have food, maybe even salmon, since this was fishing season.

Kyoti waited around for a while and finally asked, "Where are all the People?"

One of them answered by asking what Kyoti meant.

"Well, I would like to talk to your headman," Kyoti said very seriously.

Actually Kyoti just wanted to eat. Kyoti was starving.

They both laughed. "What headman. Hey, man, where'd you come from?" one of them asked.

Kyoti kinda got mad then and answered, "I came walking up the river. I never saw any People. All I been seeing is those Swallows and they sure got lots of houses. Now you talk to me in their talk and laugh at me. I'm hungry and you don't even offer me anything to eat."

Well that shamed them guys out. Even though they weren't quite sure of what Kyoti was talking about. One of them said, "Cheeze, you coulda just said that in the first place. We're Indians. Come on, we'll go over to the house and feed you up."

So that was how Kyoti got to Nespelum. Kyoti got to meet one old person there that talked right. All the rest of the People just kept talking Swallow talk. They used words in Swallow that didn't have a meaning that Kyoti could figure out.

What was the most surprising was that all the people lived in Swallow houses and ate Swallow food. A whole lot of things were pretty strange.

Kyoti had looked and looked for somebody who could talk in the People's language. Kyoti asked the one person who could talk proper, how this had all happened.

The person was a very old woman. Kyoti recognized her name

and knew which family and village her People were from. She was from an old headman family.

She looked at Kyoti for quite a while and recognized Kyoti. Then she cried and cried for a long time. "Kyoti," she said, "I never thought you was ever going to come back. Things haven't been good for quite a while now. I kept hoping you would show up. Them Swallows came. We don't know what happened. They did lots of things. They built that thing across the river again, like when they were Monster people and you broke their dams to bring the salmon up. I don't think it's made out of spit and clay like that other time, but it's made something like that. They did lots of other worse stuff. How come you never came back for a long time? Now look what happened."

Kyoti was quiet for a while. "Well I guess I went to sleep for a while. You know sometimes I oversleep a little," Kyoti joked, trying to make her feel better.

Actually Kyoti was well known for oversleeping all the time. And actually Kyoti always used that as an excuse for being too late for something important.

But the old woman just kept crying. She kept on talking, saying, "Noboby listens to me. Nobody knows you anymore. You better go up to Vernon, up there in the North Okanagan. Go see Tommy, he keeps telling people about you. Maybe he can tell you something about what happened."

So Kyoti continued on up the river, stopping at each village. This time they were easy to find, now that Kyoti knew that the People had moved into Swallow homes. They were easy to find because they looked different than the way Swallows kept their houses. The People didn't seem to care to keep up the houses the way the Swallows worked at it, day in day out, non-stop until they dropped dead. That was no surprise. They weren't Swallows.

Kyoti tried to talk to some of the headmen. Kyoti would suggest something like, "You should break them Swallow dams, and let the salmon come back. They know where to come, they never forget. I told them not to. You shouldn't eat that Swallow food. Look at all the sick People."

Actually Kyoti himself was getting pretty sick and gaunt from eating stuff that didn't taste or look like food. Especially real food like fresh salmon.

But the headman would just shake his head and say, "Get out of here, Kyoti. Your kind of talk is just bullshit. If you say them things People will get riled up and they might start to raise hell. They might even try to do something stupid like break the dams. Them Swallows get mad real easy. Besides, we'll just end up looking stupid. We gotta work with them now even if we don't exactly like what they do. We gotta survive. We gotta get money to buy food and other things. We gotta have jobs to live. That's how it is now, we can't go back to old times. We need them Swallows, they're smart. They know lots that we don't know about. They know how to live right. We just got to try harder to be like them. So get outta here. You're not real anyway. You're just a dream of the old People."

They would say things like that even while they talked right face-to-face to Kyoti. Even when Kyoti was right there in front of them.

Kyoti would walk on feeling real bad. Kyoti had seen lots of People in really bad shape. They walked around with their minds hurt. They couldn't see or hear good anymore. Their bodies were poisoned. They didn't care much for living anymore. They thought they were Swallows, but couldn't figure out why the Swallows taunted and laughed at them. They couldn't seem to see how the Swallows stole anything they could pick up for their houses, how they took over any place and shitted all over it, not caring because they could just fly away to another place. They couldn't seem to see that the Swallow treated them just as they pleased without any respect.

Kyoti could see that them Swallows were still a Monster people. They were pretty tricky making themselves act like they were People but all the while, underneath, being really selfish Monsters that destroy People and things like rivers and mountains. Now Kyoti could see the reason for being awakened early. There was work to be done. It was time to change the Swallows from Monsters into something that didn't destroy things. Kyoti was Kyoti and that was the work Kyoti had to do.

Eventually Kyoti came to a place where a young one was sitting by the river. This young one greeted Kyoti properly in People talk. He looked at Kyoti's staff and asked politely, "Who are you, old one? I know all the old People in the Okanagan. I haven't seen you before, but you look like somebody I must have known before."

Kyoti sat down and then said, "You look like somebody I once knew. An old chief. He was really a big important chief. He was so important that he took care of People all up and down the whole Okanagan. He never kept a single salmon for himself if somebody needed it. Me, I'm just a traveller. I move around a lot when I'm not sleeping. Never know where I'll be tomorrow. I'm looking for Tommy, I guess."

The young man said, "Tommy? The old man? Yeah you must mean him. Some of us call him our chief now. It was Tommy told my mom to make sure that I was to sit here and watch the river, every day during salmon-run time.

"You see he knows that I'm a chief of the Kettle Falls. I'm a Salmon Chief, but no salmon come up here now, and there is no falls there anymore. My great grandfather was the last Salmon Chief to see the salmon come up the river. The Swallows came after that. Now I wait here and watch the river, like my father and his father before him did. They died without seeing one salmon come up the river.

"I guess I will keep on waiting. I believe Tommy when he says that we got to not give up. Sometimes I think I will see them coming. Shining and in clean water. I close my eyes during salmon-run time, and I see them. Millions of salmon coming up the river. I see my People singing, all coming down to the river to be with me, to eat again what we were given to eat. But then I open my eyes and nothing is ever there. I'm so tired and so all alone here. Nobody else cares."

So that was when Kyoti took out the shining rainbow ribbons and hung them on his staff.

Kyoti walked up to Tommy's door and said, "Tommy, open the door. I have come to talk to you. I'm going to ask you to get the People together. The ones who can hear. Tell them that I am back. You know all of them. I am going to break the dams. I'm hungry and that young one at the river has waited long enough. All my children will eat salmon again."

Kyoti shook the staff and the ground shook, too, as Tommy came out the door facing east. You shoulda seen Tommy's face, when he saw Kyoti and the rainbow ribbons hanging on the staff.

That story happened. I tell you that much. It's a powerful one. I tell it now because it's true.

Sometimes I think of that story and that morning at Owl Rock, when I see rainbow colours in the oil slicks along the river, during salmon-run time in the Okanagan, and I feel the ground shake ever so little.

MAURICE KENNY

Rain

I was only visiting that part of the country.

The Pontiac sped along the back road north of Albuquerque toward the Pueblo village of Santa Ana. I rode with an elderly Laguna Indian woman, her younger daughter who had married an Arab pedlar, her granddaughter who had married an Englishman and her great-grandson who was then too young to marry.

The road edged the rising mountains to the east and the vast mesa to the west. Through the windshield I spotted an ancient pick-up. Two figures stood near it. As we approached the truck I could see an old Indian couple selling melons. The man held one up to us in silence.

In the Pontiac all three women smoked; the young boy drank a Coke. I was thirsty myself for the sweet juices of those melons.

"They look good."

Too late. The driver passed the truck without a thought.

"What kind of melons are those?" I asked.

The conversation already in progress was so intent upon the trip's purpose, our destination, that no one heard me.

"Those Santa Anas are going to dance a rain, I tell you," the elderly Laguna woman announced emphatically.

"I believe you're right, Grandma," replied the young driver.

"Mercy! Hope they do. This heat's a killer. Good thing the car's air-conditioned, or I'd be wilted for sure."

"The juice of those melons back there would have cooled us off," I offered, but received no response.

"We gonna see 'em dance, Gramma?"

"We sure are. See them dance the very rain down, Sonny."

I come from rain country. I want rain or snow then to relieve the unbearable heat and the dry sage stench of the desert.

"Alma, when we get there park the car behind the pueblo."

"Right. I'll let you folks out first. And take Sonny with you."

We approached a narrow bridge spanning the Rio Grande River, which was nearly dry. Barely more than a trickle seeped to the Mexican border at Juarez. A long line of cars and trucks waited at the far end of the bridge to cross.

"Folks are leaving!"

"Hope we're not too late!"

"No. Grandma. They dance all afternoon . . . same as they do at Laguna."

"Oh! They are going to dance down a rain, I tell you."

The elderly woman's face shone with something like ecstatic joy.

"That's power, Grandma."

"That's power, Alma."

"They got power all right."

"We gonna see 'em dance, Gramma?"

"Yes, Sonny, we are going to see the Santa Anas dance down the rain from the sunny sky up there."

"Is there gonna be a rainbow, Gramma?"

"Rainbows all over the desert."

I come from country where it is not necessary to dance rain or look for rainbows in the sky.

"Alma, you park behind the pueblo. Margo, you go get me a big piece of frybread with honey when we get there. Sonny, you come with me to the plaza. They'll find us. We can't get lost in little Santa Ana. I want to be there up front to see them dance that rain," the great-grandmother proclaimed.

Beyond the adobe village an acre of corn, knee-high, sun-soaked, roots scrambling to the the river to suck what tricklets of water remained in the August beds. Overhead the clear sky waited for passing clouds. A citron hue creased the horizon.

We unloaded three metal fold-up chairs and an umbrella from

the car trunk. Alma drove off to the parking lot. We others headed for the plaza.

At the pueblo edge a Ferris wheel whirled. Music of a merry-go-round tinkled the afternoon. Sonny's face brightened with surprise, but his grandmother grasped his hand tightly. A smell of burning charcoal seamed the air. Young boys weaved in and out of the strolling crowds selling containers of Coca-Cola from large wooden crates. Children, including Sonny, stared hungrily at the various booths selling cotton candy on plastic sticks. A tongue slid along the rim of a lip. Hundreds of people milled between craft stands and beverage counters, charcoal pits where great cauldrons of bubbling grease singed brown tortilla-like bread. Flies swarmed about the honey pots. A leathery-skinned man wavered through the crowds hawking balloons: purple, the colour of his lips; yellow as the sun; blue as the clear sky; red as the heat of the afternoon.

We waded through the carnival atmosphere.

In the village groups of people loitered in the plaza itself and on the roofs of the squat adobe houses framing the dusty plaza crammed with the curious. Most people had brought folding chairs and umbrellas to ward off the sun's rays and the rain, should it fall. A man raked the dust clean of the central plaza readying the grounds for the dancers.

People, old friends and new, chattered like mice between bites of greasy frybread with rich honey and sips of Coke. A little girl dressed in bright yellow with matching silk panties showing sat on the dust. A damp spot moved from under her. Two arms reached down and plucked her away as though she were a lemon hanging from a tree.

I was a stranger in that part of the country.

"There's Milly Velarde over there . . ."

"Jim must have brought her from Cuberio."

". . . right under the portico of that adobe, I'm going to bid afternoon."

"Be careful, Mother. These kids might knock you down the way they're running so carelessly. No respect!"

"Can I go?"

"No, Sonny, you stay here with me. Your Mama'll be here in a minute. Doesn't take long to park a car. My, it is hot. I hope these Santa Anas *do* dance rain. I certainly do. Cool us off a little bit."

By then my mouth was clotted with dust. My bare arms, face slowly covered with a fine red film; sweat spotted my shirt.

"Alma! Oh, Alma, over here."

Our driver, the younger woman, had entered the plaza.

Dancers began lining up at the narrow entrance of the plaza between the adobe huts. Women and little girls wore black dresses with red sashes. High wooden tiaras reared from atop their heads over loose black hair. The tiaras had cut-outs of stars and crescent moons. The women carried cedar boughs and boughs were attached to arm bands. The men and young boys were dressed in white kilts with a coyote pelt falling behind, and a wide rope sash circled the waist. Beads hung down their chests. Within turquoise arm bands cedar twigs were entwined. They carried gourd rattles. All the dancers were painted in vermilion.

One older man stood off from the thronging group. He held what appeared a flag pole from which streamed coloured pennants. An old woman, obviously the lead dancer, sucked an orange ice cone. She wore faded green tennis shoes while other dancers were all barefoot. She, however, was dressed as the other women and carried boughs of cedar in her hands as did the other women.

"You want a drink of something?" Alma asked. "It's boiling!"

"Broiling," I nodded.

"Oh, glory, yes, Alma. Get Sonny a Coke, too."

"Can I go with you, Mama?"

"Stay with your grandmother so you don't get lost."

Sadly the little fellow sat down on the dusty earth . . . with the sounds of the merry-go-round tinkling in his ears.

A heavy-set old man relaxed into a folding chair next to us. His eyes were rheumy. He was blind. A little boy of three or four stood between his grandfather's parted knees. Both were mailed with silver jewellery.

"It was Milly Velarde, Margo! We had a great talk." The elderly grandmother returned. "Says she's losing sight. Cataracts. But wouldn't miss these Santa Anas for the world."

"Cause they always dance rain."

"All knows we need it," pronounced the matriarch.

"Did you get a look at that river? Oh, my! . . . Look! A hawk."

"A hawk?"

"A red-tail."

"Good sign."

"When they gonna start, Grandma?"

"Soon, Sonny, soon."

"I'm hot, Grandma."

"We're all hot, Sonny."

"Alma isn't here yet, Margo? How long's it take to park a car?"

"She's here. She went to get us a cool drink of something."

The old couple selling the melons along the highway flashed into my mind, my thirst, my heat.

"She'd better hurry. The dancers are lined up to start. And the drummers. Aren't they beautiful?"

"Just beautiful, Mother."

I am a stranger in this rainless country.

I am visiting from a land where it is never necessary to dance rain from the clouds. I thirst for sweet waters of the melons the old woman picked from her wild vines growing on the mesa floor, this dry desert. I am a stranger, but I will wait for the sky to open and flood the plaza, the outer fields with rain. I will wait for the rain to sting my arms, to wet my dry face, to cool my flesh.

"They're about to commence."

A stranger, I spied six men dressed in white shirts and pants join the waiting, anxious dancers immobile assembled into two straight lines . . . female and male.

"Here comes Alma. You should have gone with her, Sonny. She is burdened will all those Coke containers."

"I wanted to Grandma, but . . ."

"Not much ice in these things. Won't cool you off much. But they're wet."

"That's what's important," Margo commented.

The chatting, the noise of the plaza hushed low. Only the tinkle of the merry-go-round corrupted the silence. We sat there as if figures in portrait, a photograph.

I remember McIntosh growing on the trees back home in my own grandmother's backyard, and my grandfather's transparents hanging in his now deserted orchard.

I think of spring waters gurgling, spouting from rocky hillsides of low-mountain country of home, north. I think of wading in clear creeks coolly wending their journey toward rivers. I think of rain which will flood those same rivers rushing to the great lake which in turn will empty its belly contents into the sea.

The photo remains static. The sun sweats . . . the only movement of the moment. The sun steadily rises in the sky. It swirls before my gaze, my brain. It beats upon my face with hot hands. My shirt grows moist, my face cakes with dust.

I am a stranger in this part of the country. And I am sitting here under this burning sun waiting for the Santa Ana dancers to bring rain onto my hair, the mesa cactus, the river, which is nearly empty, the corn, which is still green yet slowly parching for want of rain and which will die and the people will go into winter without corn.

The photo blurs.

Each June my mother would gather her young brood as though we were a flock of chicks and go off to a distant meadow. She spent the day teaching her children the rites of wild berry picking. She would show us how to squeeze the strawberries and drink the juices under the summer sun, juices which ran between our fingers, down our arms like blood from open wounds, and through the crevice between our usually naked toes. We licked the flesh in laughter, our thirst assuaged. We spent our childhood in berry fields and brambles. My mother, however, remains allergic to strawberries.

Later in the summer she would haul us off to the blackberry brambles, the raspberries whose thorns clutched the skin and stung our hands with nasty bites and tears. Then blueberries, currants, gooseberries, elderberries of the woods. Berry after berry until we had gleaned the land and the wild fruit filled our bellies and filled glass jars for winter on the shelves in the cellar.

Rain sweeps across the hills in spring. Furious April floods the valleys. Meadows run black and treacherous with rainwater. The laundry barrels overflow, cisterns gurgle joyfully. Children play naked in the yard. The stench of enclosure, of winter hibernation, is washed from the flesh. We wait for berrytime.

Eventually, slowly the rivers retrench. Creeks babble again. Hay grows tall to the sun, and chicory wheat, corn, alfalfa shoots to the eye. Squash and bean vines start a steady crawl across the earth. Cows are contented; birds sing. Bears are happy with summer honey. Fox trek across open spaces, tails low to the ground, eyes fixed on a sparrow. Chipmunks race the edge of stone walls of a cemetery. Woodchucks munch grass growing thick and sweet in the open meadow. Then August starts to brown. Wild grapes cluster and purple on vines at the fence.

In my father's pasture an old plum tree hangs heavy with fruit. I taste the sweetness of flesh. It is an old tree, tall and scraggly with few limbs and not many leaves. The dark fruit is delicious. And a pole will bring the fruit down into the hand.

In the winter old men will nibble dried currants and smoke a mixture of sumac and cedar and red willow in their pipes. Women will talk of the largest wild strawberry ever picked thereabouts. Children will crack and chomp the meat of hickory nuts gathered on the floor of the autumn woods. Or pop corn.

The blurred photo swims into focus again.

Sun burns my hair.

I am a stranger here. I have never seen rain danced.

The dancers are about to start.

The drummers are ready.

In the vast, far distance Mount Taylor broods obsidic and tall and heavy against the horizon. A single cloud hovers above the peak. The mountain's sovereign power dominates the desert mesa which appears empty.

The sun blazes, burning flesh and earth.

Men beat drums. The dancers slowly proceed into the plaza. The man lifting the guidon of pennants follows. Two single lines of dancers . . . women, men follow the lead woman in the green tennis shoes. Their faces are stained red. The men's chests are stained blue. The cedar forests of arms move into the centre of the pueblo. Bare feet kick up puffs of red dust. Men shake rattles. Drummers drum. The guidon lowers. Drummers drum even, loud, incessantly. The sun hovers. Light falls upon Mount Taylor. The dark cloud has moved off the mountain peak. The dark mesa clears. Dancers move across the plaza before a silent horde of people. Minutes pass, perhaps hours. No one counts time because time is neither recognizable nor of any importance. The dancers move, interchanging, stepping forwards, backwards, weaving, drumming the earth with their naked feet. Men slide between women to regroup another line. Rattles shake. The guidon lowers again to the earth, the dry dust, yet refuses to touch the earth. Drums drum. Brown bodies shine in the sweat of the dance. Paint melts on the flesh. The sun grudgingly moves before the cloud. The photo is animated before the fierce disbelieving eyes of the crowd.

The sweet smell of burning sage permeates the air.

The crowd is still, breathless. Gnats hang onto the fetid air. The cloud moves.

Drums drum.

A shadow crosses the dancers' faces and the crowd under the umbrellas in the adobe pueblo of the mesa.

Drums drum.

The guidon lowers.

Rattles rattle.

I am a stranger in this part of the country.

Rattles rattle.

The guidon lowers but still does not touch the red, dusty earth.

"They sure have power in this pueblo," the matriarch exclaims.

"That's power, Grandmother."

The blind old grandfather sitting with his grandson between his parted knees relaxes in his folding chair, his face to the sky, to the cloud, to the expected rain. He turns the boy's face with his mutton hands to the sky. He mumbles a prayer to himself and then into the ear of the little boy, and to the impending rain. Perhaps he remembers his own youth, his own dance in that plaza year and years before when his feet were strong and supple, not swollen as now, when his rheumy eyes sparkled with expectancy and could watch the cloud move across the quivering mesa to the pueblo, when his hands shook the rattles, the paint smeared and running down his chest naked to the falling pellets of cool rain, and his arms were festooned with the boughs bound in turquoise bands. He smiled a slight grin showing old teeth the colour of dried corn, but the smile changes into a dark frown as his ear catches the din of the carnival outside the plaza with the music of the merry-go-round vying with the beat of the drums, the rattles, and the pounding feet of the dancers. What chance has rain with this mechanical noise frightening the cloud and the spirits of the sky. His own grandchild begging for cotton candy and a swirl on the Ferris wheel. His people stuffing themselves with hot dogs and Cokes. Changes. Everything changes now. He was glad to be blind. One day soon he would be deaf. Yet, before that biological change he would start the little boy learning the steps, the shake of the rattle, help him to prepare the costume, hunt his coyote, with bow and arrow, and teach him how to forge the bands to bind the cedar to the arm muscle. The boy would learn.

The child stood between the knees of his grandfather shaking a clenched but empty fist as the rain slowly dropped from the sky.

"Power! That's power," the elderly Laguna woman whispered.

The lead dancer in the green tennis shoes falls out of line and accepts a drink of water from a girl at the edge of the plaza.

Feet move and shuffle.

Red and blue paint run sweaty flesh, mingle, drip to the dust puffing up and flying away from the dry earth.

"Power," whisper the voices in the plaza.

The long two lines of dancers stand like falling raindrops caught in the eye of the camera, a photograph.

Whispers breathe across the plaza, the small village of adobe houses with the beat of the drum and the soft shuffle of feet and the rattle of the gourds.

I am a stranger here in this part of the country.

I sniff the burning sage.

I feel the first drop of rain strike my hot cheek, my earlobe, feel it slide through wisps of my hair.

The old woman in the green tennis shoes leads her dancers into the falling rain.

Dust settles. The dancers' feet cake with mud.
Drums drum.
Rattles rattle.
Rain.

The old grandfather is first to stand. He folds his chair, places his hand in the small fist of his grandson, and urges the boy to lead him from the plaza.

At the roadside I buy a melon. The vendor cuts it into small wedges. I suck the sweet juices, and taste my grandmother's McIntosh, my mother's strawberries, my father's plums. I buy three more melons from the couple at the side of the road and take them back to Albuquerque.

"They sure can dance down the rain in that Santa Ana village."

"Sure can, Mother."

"Mama, there's a rainbow."

"The tail . . ."

And there was.

Down the road a few yards ahead of us walked the old grandfather and the boy in stumbling gate. I watched him turn onto a path leading deep into the mesa as the Pontiac passed and sped on.

I am a stranger to this country. I'm visiting a short while.

JOAN CRATE

Welcome to the Real World

Mother pours tea into a green mug and sets it in front of me on the flowered plastic tablecloth. The petals match the flecks of yellow and green on the arborite countertop Uncle Teddy installed so many years ago, and the countertop goes with the yellow kitchen tile and the avocado stove and fridge. I remember when they bought that stove and fridge. We had propane before, and one winter Keith, who was on the wagon and had to keep busy, decided to do us a favour and rewire our kitchen. It took forever because Keith didn't really know what he was doing, and Mother kept having to phone Uncle Teddy who's an electrician for advice, most of which Keith ignored. While Keith was busy with books and diagrams, advice from friends, and strange buzzing, rotating, thick-handled tools, the air stung with suspense.

"The Marvel of Electricity" was the title of one of the chapters in my science book at school. No matter how practical and simplistic the explanations in the text tried to be, electricity, like rain and tides and the reaction of vinegar with baking soda, was inexplicable and magical. I watched Keith fumble through papers, scratch his oily head, and stare at the tools in his hands with glazed, red eyes. He didn't know how to start, or was afraid to start; I wasn't sure which.

One day Father came home and methodically laid the drawings, the books, Uncle Teddy's electric drill, Keith's wire cutter, the screwdrivers with assorted heads and different coloured handles – red, green, orange, clear plastic, and black – out on the table, and drew his big hands over them; then he read the instructions on one of the diagrams. His voice was low and grave, as if he were beginning a story. The green wire is the ground wire. Make sure this wire is always connected first before proceeding with the other wires. Like colours must be connected, for example, white with white, black with black, yellow with yellow. Connections should be wrapped securely with electrician's tape, or capped. See insert. The green wire is always the ground wire. White with white, black with black, yellow with yellow, Father chanted. He bowed his head. The green wire is the ground wire. Keith entered the kitchen and Father turned to him. Like colours are to be connected, he told him. And after the joining is made, it must be wrapped securely with electrician's tape, black. Keith nodded solemnly and I remembered how electricity was part of the spirit of Thunder, and Thunder was a man, long ago before the earth was changed.

Thunder was married to Rain, and their children were Snow and Hail. But the Changer transformed our world to make it the way it is today, and Thunder and his family were sent to live in the sky where they rule over the weather.

"Rain, rain, go away, come again another daaaay, Jewell and I sang at the window. "It's raaaaiiining, it's poooouuuring, the old man is snoooooring. He went to bed and bumped his head, and couldn't get up in the moooorning."

"Wain, wain," Crow bleated, tottering beside us.

I screwed my eyes tight and pressed my cheek against the cold window. "Please, Rain!" I pleaded. "Oh, please stop by tomorrow, oh, please. You can come some other time, at night maybe, or the day after tomorrow, but tomorrow is the picnic, and I want to run in the races. Oh, please God, let me win the races."

They were very sad to leave the earth, their home, so the Changer promised Rain, Snow, and Hail that they could visit it when their hearts grew heavy. But Thunder himself was not allowed to fall from the sky: his power was too great.

Sunny was only five or so then, but he was always underfoot, turning the drill on and charging at the walls, peeling the plastic coating back on the broken wires that littered the kitchen floor, twisting the copper strands together and wrapping clumps of black tape around them. "See, see," he'd hold them proudly up to Father or Keith.

The Changer took some of Thunder's spirit and scattered it over the earth. It will be called electricity, he said.

One night when I came downstairs to go to the bathroom, I saw Mother at the kitchen table. She had cleared the spot in front of her of copper wires, plaster, and screwdrivers, and sat looking through pamphlets with black line drawings of electric fridges and stoves. The thin line of her mouth had softened; she smiled faintly.

The next day Uncle Teddy arrived and in one uneventful hour he rewired our kitchen. Mother and Sunny were jubilant, but I felt cheated. Quietly I stole into the back porch where Keith was packing up his books and diagrams, the coloured screwdrivers, his wire cutter and hand drill. We wrapped them in newspaper and placed them in his cardboard box with the same ceremony that Father had laid them on the kitchen table a week earlier, with the same solemnity that Jewell and I had lifted the Christmas baubles off the tree and tucked them into a slotted carton the month before. I wanted to say something about the electricity being here all along: all Uncle Teddy did was find it, but I didn't know how to start. Instead we both remained silent amidst the crinkling newspaper.

When it was time to choose the colour of the new appliances, Jewell and I offered our suggestions. She wanted Harvest Gold, though it was the name she liked much more than the actual shade. "Harvest Gold," she repeated over and over. "Gold," lingering over each letter. Gold lamé gowns – the kind starlets pictured in *Hollywood and How* magazine wore – waltzed through her thoughts while I tried to persuade Mother to order Burnished Copper. The words gleamed with Aztec skin and old suns. Young virgins squirmed under knife blades on stone tables. "It was their own fault," Jewell had commented. "They should have screwed their heads off. That would have saved them."

"No." Mother finally passed judgement on our choices. "Too yellow," and "too dark." It was Avocado Green she chose.

"Had one helluva time finding this place," one of the Simpsons-Sears men said when they delivered the enormous crates to our house. It was before all the houses appeared on the Ridge and no one lived on either side of us for half a mile or so. Once the new fridge and stove were out of their packing, Mother wiped them lovingly with a cloth dipped in vinegar water, and Jewell and I and even little Crow and Sunny paraded in front of them, oohing and ahhing. Now they look old. The fridge, much smaller than my almond two-door, isn't even frost-free, and the stove clock has been broken for years. I don't think they even make avocado anymore. But Mother still keeps them gleaming with some sort of appliance wax she buys from the Fuller Brush man.

Strong fingers pull a strand of hair from my face. She sighs and looks at me wistfully. "Dione," she says, "something is wrong."

Age has opened Mother's face, but I remember when we sat on the living-room floor with Father, how she moved in, cleaning with swift circles around us, how her face was a locked door. When the living room was dusted and polished, she'd stride busily into the kitchen and clatter plates together and bang pots and pans. At night when we sat on the double bed Jewell and I shared, she'd pound up the steps and start loading laundered sheets into the linen closet across the hall, her mouth a grey fold in her face.

"Filling their heads with dreams!" she'd huff, or "welcome to the real world," when Father finished. That was it, always anger.

Her own allusions to the past were short and often brutal. "When I was a girl, Auntie Emma and I had to keep our rooms spotless or The Grand took her broom to us. And you think I'm fussy!" Or, "The Grand Führer strapped us if we so much as dropped a fork at the dinner table."

It was Father of course who had first coined these names for our grandparents, and we referred to them this way always, although there was some embarrassment during our first visit to the Grand Manor when I looked up at the big-bellied, hard-eyed man who was my grandfather and mumbled, horrified, "You're the Grand Führer." Fortunately since I was four, the mumbled title sounded like Gran Fur and, Mother quickly offered, was supposed to be Grandfather.

Mother snatches Elijah from my arms and raises him up above her smiling face. "Whasa matter? Mommy not payin' any attention to a liddle baby?" She lowers his wet lips to hers and kisses him with sharp nips. Her mouth, relaxed, is fuller than it used to be, and her dowdy brown hair has faded to a soft grey. She turns to me. "Dione, I know it's not easy, starting out." I drop my glance from her face and look into my tea. On the brown surface I see an enormous nose and small, lowered eyes.

I'm sure it wasn't easy for my mother. Grand Führer, a strict military man, and the very proper Grand had not been prepared for their eldest daughter to take up with a half-breed from the wilds of the West Coast. They refused to attend the wedding, and did not speak to Mother until after Jewell was born. For years they refused to allow Father in their house, and Mother would not visit them, would speak to them only if they telephoned. Auntie Emma became the messenger between parents and daughter, according to Jewell who remembers, trying to reason with both parties but most sympathetic to Mother. After all, the Grands hadn't been that impressed with Uncle Teddy either, though they did pay for his and Emma's wedding.

But as the Grands grew older, their opposition to Father softened, we were invited over on Boxing Day, and often at Easter and Thanksgiving. When Father was away at camp, Mother took us over to swim in their pool, yet the Grands remained strange to Jewell and me and we were never comfortable around them. Perhaps they had spent too much of our lives as disembodied voices over the telephone, the cause of unhappy whisperings between Mother and Auntie Emma in the kitchen, and dissension between Mother and Father. They were stiff and formal around Father and never laughed at his jokes. If only he'd tell them a story, I thought, then they'd understand.

"Isn't there an awful lot of rain on the Queen Charlottes?" the Grand asked Father after he had returned from there. "I don't know how the people can put up with it. As if Vancouver isn't bad enough."

It wasn't always like that, he told her. In the early days the islands were dry and fire tore through the big-trunked trees and destroyed the villages. The people were always having to rebuild or relocate, and often lives were lost in the flames. Rain was what the people wanted, to dampen the bone-dry ground and quench the trees. The room crackled, and I glanced at Jewell, sitting next to me on the couch the Grand called "settee," but she wouldn't return my gaze; she stared straight ahead, self-conscious, her features burned away by the light flaring through the window. There were so many windows in that room, small panes of leaded glass with foggy boarders that blurred the trees and flowering bushes in the huge yard. I stared outside, his words falling around me like rain.

Rain came. Not that moment, nor that day. But it came that season, falling through the forest, feeding the trees and earth. It was the answer to prayers and pleas, the wish made on the beached whale. The people rescued it where it struggled not far from shore. The whale allowed the people one wish and they wished for rain. The trees grew bigger and more numerous, and in the thick forests many animals thrived.

Rain shimmered on the carpet, on the settee, and the room was hushed except for the gentle chant of rain. Dusk crept through the window, cupped Jewell's glistening face and sharpened the Grand's features. We all sat silently, even Crow in Mother's arms, even Mother. Almost smiling, she watched Father. The Grand's eyes were distant. Then she sat up with a start. "What? Oh, yes, are you finished your tall tale?"

Finally the Grand Manor was sold and the two of them moved to Florida. Now they send postcards with pictures of long, white beaches and coloured beach umbrellas. At Christmas we get a package of dried fruit, pecans, American cigarettes, and sweatshirts for Crow and Sunny with sayings like, "My Grandmother went to Florida and all she got me was this stupid sweatshirt," and "Sun of a Beach," and we all get money, except Jewell since she got married. Except me now.

Elijah drools over Mother's shoulder as she burps him. "Are you sure you're all right?"

"Yes." I sip at the distorted brown face moving farther down the cup.

Is Joseph treating you well?" Mother refuses to say Jo-Jo. Too childish, she says, for a grown man, and she can't seem to remember Jorges, even though I've been over the pronunciation with her many times. Yor-gos, yor-gos, I tell her. Just think of "your ghost," but she doesn't like that and I don't bother to correct her anymore.

"Oh, there he goes," she says, touching the wet patch spreading over Elijah's thigh.

I pull the change pad out of the diaper bag, lay it on the table and Mother hands me Elijah. He looks up at me with glittering blue eyes, dark as a stormy sea, a troubled sky. I close my eyes and rub my hand over his tummy, soft as velvet, and pinch his chubby thighs and calves. Together we laugh, and Mother joins in. Warm, he's warm, his small body smooth and warm, and I scoop him up and hold him to me, warm and tiny, so very tiny.

"He's got a bit of a diaper rash," Mother says, her eyes on his soft little bum.

"It just came up," I offer. "And the cream I've got doesn't seem to be doing anything." As I rub a Baby Clean over him, his little body gives a sudden jerk and his face puckers into a sob. "There, there," I whisper. "There, there." He listens to my voice. "It's all right. Mommy's gonna put some Vaseline on that poor little bum. There, there."

"You need zinc ointment," Mother advises. "It's the best. Why don't you try Isaac's on your way home."

"Okay." I snap him into a clean sleeper. "There, there," and settle him at my breast. "Poor little baby, poor little baby." My fingers move circles over his cheeks.

I ask Mother how Sunny and Crow are doing.

"Sunny's got a job at the Turbo. Started just last week. Says he wants to buy a car next year. And he's still doing that go-cart business on weekends. I think the little bugger's smoking. Won't tell me. Hides it. No time for schoolwork, of course; you know Sunny." She gives an exasperated sigh and lights up a cigarette. "Crow's still at the A&W, but getting bored. She was wondering if you could get her on at the Rimrock Cafeteria? What do you think?"

The Rimrock Cafeteria. Where I first watched Jo-Jo and Linda through the window in the kitchen door. "I'll see what I can do," I tell her. "And how's her school?"

"Well, same old story with Crow, you know. Teachers always say she could be doing better. Doesn't put enough effort into it.

Loves drama though. Oh, I forgot to tell you, she's got the lead role or something in a play for the North Shore Drama Festival. Says she's writing the songs for it, too. Still can't complain. Mostly B's on her report."

"Stay and see them," Mother pleads as I tie Elijah's bonnet. "They'll want to see you."

"I wish I could, but Jo-Jo's coming home early. He's got a meeting tonight about this new hotel deal down on the water." I peck her cheek. I want to see them, too. I'm just not ready.

"Don't forget Isaac's," she calls out to me. "My, but isn't it a nice day!" The sunlight bleaches away the lines around her eyes and mouth. "Bye," she waves as I place Elijah in his car seat.

▲

RICHARD G. GREEN

The Last Raven

Looking at Dan and Nola Goupil, you'd never guess they're married. Not that they're unworthy but she's at least two heads taller which makes you wonder how they make out physically. They subtly administer the word of God each week, while we sit in a circle trying to overcome hardness from the high-backed wooden chairs. This circle is part of a continuing plot to get us closer to God, nature, and each other by moulding us into a team of young-adult Christians. Truth is, Sunday school attendance is mandatory to play on the hockey team, which is why I'm here.

When I adjust my tie clasp, my elbow presses against the flesh of a bare-armed girl sitting beside me. She brushes at the spot as if removing bacteria, folds her hands with kindergarten precision, and places them in her lap. She knows I'm Mohawk and I know that's why she brushed off her arm. Girls outnumber boys two-to-one in this class, and none of them drives you mad with desire.

"Well, Mr. Silverheels," Nola says, her voice one octave above a whisper in true Christian fashion. "What do you think the meaning of Christ's action toward the penitent woman at the home of Simon the Pharisee was?" Hanging *Mr.* and *Miss* to surnames is supposed to elevate us to adult status, though we're expected to call Dan and Nola by their given names. When the Goupils first arrived, I labelled this a get-acquainted trick, but I accept their eccentricities, though it's wierd not being called Jim.

"What?" I say. "I . . . I don't think I heard the question." I glance toward Bill Shostrom, as he flashes a devilish smile. He slouches in his chair, the lapels of his blue suit flex into a diamond shape exposing the too short length of his polka-dotted tie. His punk hair is greasy with hair-goo, and a glimmer from the ceiling lamp reflects off his forehead. If you believe opposites attract, then you know why we're chums.

Tracking the direction of my eyes, Nola says: "Now don't you tell him the answer, Mr. Shostrom." The class laughs. She turns to the fat girl beside me, who's impatiently waving an arm.

"Yes, Miss Breen."

Miss Breen leaps to her feet. "I think it's a story to remind us that even though we're constantly submerged in sin," she says, confidence rampant in her tone, "Christ loves those who love." Satisfied with her brief moment of superiority, she directs a smirk toward me as she plops her oversized buttocks back into the chair.

"I disagree," I say. I'm not sure why this blurted out, but now I'm committed to explanation. I feel tension in the wily shifting of everybody's eyes.

Dan Goupil glares at me, and a nervous hush settles over the room. He never enters class discussion, but I can see he's interpreted my remark as an attack on his wife. He removes a handkerchief, holds his plastic-rimmed glasses toward the ceiling light, and huffs on the lenses. Wiping them with a fluid motion he says quietly, "Exactly what do you disagree with, Mr. Silverheels?" A smile curls his thin lips as he scans the class. "Surely you don't challenge the love of Jesus, eh?"

"No sir," I say.

"Well I'm glad to hear that." The class translates his actions, and, suddenly, I'm in a sea of snickering faces. "Well then, Mr. Silverheels." He put on his glasses. "*What* do you disagree with?"

"It's just that . . . well, I uh, I don't think the love of Jesus is in question here. That's the constant theme of the New Testament and is indicated in many previous occasions. I think that, by forgiving this woman of all her sins, Christ is directing a lesson of humility toward Simon."

"Humility?"

"Yes. He's raised Mary Magdalen to a level of respectability above that of His host. He's used her to show Simon that her example of love makes her superior."

"You think Christ would *use* somebody for His own gain?"

"In this case, yes."

All eyes rest upon Dan. It's plain that emphasis has shifted from correct and incorrect and is now a question of vanity. To these people, Christ is their saviour; to me, He's a prophet. I realize Dan's next statement decides the outcome. He glances at his wristwatch, and I'm reminded that it's almost time for dismissal. Perhaps I'll be saved by the bell.

Nola raises her eyes above an opened Bible. "Mr. Silverheels?" she asks. "What do you think Christ means when He says, 'Therefore I tell you her sins, which are many, are forgiven for she loved much; but he who is forgiven little, loves little.'"

Dan brushes dandruff specs from his lapel. Simultaneously, shuffling feet and voices penetrate from the corridor outside. Looking at me, Dan says, "I think you've misconstrued the point of today's lesson . . ."

"Dan," Nola smiles. "I think you're *both* right." Everybody closes their Bible, with a thump. "Now, class," Nola continues. "Before you all run off, don't forget our house-party this afternoon. We expect to have a lot of fun, and I pray none of you will miss it."

I stand and file toward the door, a feeling of betrayal welling up inside me. If the objective of this class is participation, why haven't I been shown any mercy? Passing Dan at the doorway, I smile meekly. He squeezes my shoulder and says, "See you this afternoon." But I'm unable to answer.

On our way home, Bill and me and a skinny kid named Hartmann always stop at Gimpy's Diner. Our arrangement is we keep Gimpy's shovelled in winter and he lets us in on Sundays to play a pinball machine everybody calls "The Chief." Light the 975,000 point-feather, and with Gimpy's verification you get a dollar from the "Picnic Fund" jar. In three years of play, I've won twice.

"Are you going to the Goupils' this afternoon, Jim?" Hartmann stares at my reflection in the machine's glass panel.

"Not in a million years."

"What about you, Bill?"

"I dunno. I've got a lot of homework to do."

Hartmann looks back at me. "What are you going to do?"

"I don't know," I say, tearing open my collection envelope.

"Hey," Bill says. "Your parents are supposed to take mine to a lacrosse game, eh? You're not going with them, are you?"

"No," I say. "The Warriors are in last place, and they'll probably lose again. I'll probably stay home and terrorize my sister."

"Get out of the way, amateurs." Bill squeezes between Hartmann and me. "Make way for the pro."

"Speaking of girls," Hartmann says, "maybe I'll go to the Goupils' party. Linda'll probably be there."

"Nola's kid sister?"

"Yeah."

Inserting a quarter into the slot, Bill says, "Don't tell me you're in love with Linda Switzer?" He pushes the coin-return button with the heel of his hand and takes out a jackknife. "Hey Gimpy," he works the blade into the slot. "This damn thing's jammed again!"

"I wouldn't say I was in *love* with her," Hartmann says.

Gimpy walks over, scratches his belly, and pounds on the machine. To Bill, he says, "I don't know why you're the one who always screws up this machine."

"Because he's just a big *screw*-up," I say, overcome with cleverness.

"When they get older, you gotta prime 'em a bit." Gimpy kicks the machine and the coin clinks inside. Lights flash. Bells clang. The caricature of an Indian in Sioux headdress swings his tomahawk and dances backward into starting position. "There. What did I tell ya, eh?" Gimpy winks and limps back to his cleaning chores.

"I wouldn't say I was in love with her," Hartmann repeats. "But if you guys aren't going to be doing anything," he cracks a knuckle, "then I'm going to the Goupils' party."

Bill launches his first ball. "Who says we're not going to be doing anything?" He pushes a flipper button, and a wave of satisfaction sweeps his face. "We're going to be shooting drunken crows this afternoon."

According to Bill's latest plan, after our parents leave for the lacrosse game, we're going to take our fathers' shotguns on a hunting trip. Bill says the radio reported that a flock of crows has been gathering on the edge of town menacing people for several days. Because of something called jurisdictional ingress and egress over the woods they're in, nobody can do anything about removing them.

"We're going to be big heroes, eh?" Bill says, as we leave Gimpy's. "We're going to do our duty and eliminate those hazardous crows. Meet you at the bridge at two o'clock."

When my parents leave the house, my older sister curls up on the sofa and flashes her beady eyes. "*Sehksatiyohake Senta: whah,*" she says in Mohawk. She does this to aggravate me. We left the reserve when I was three, and my family seldom speaks Mohawk here in Brantford. Sometimes, when the house is full of visitors, she gets everybody going and there's always a point where they all look at me and laugh. But she can't fool me. She wants me out of the house this afternoon, so she can cuddle with her boyfriend. She's hovering around me like a fruit fly on a puckered apple, and it's impossible to get the shotgun from my parents' closet. To avoid suspicion, I put on my new maroon windbreaker and depart for the woods in street shoes.

I'm first to arrive. I sit on my favourite girder at the railroad bridge listening to creek water gurgle far below. To the west, a band of nimbus gathers on the horizon, promising rain. Bill and Hartmann laugh while they goose-step the railroad ties, gleaming shotgun barrels propped between body and forearm. Bill wears a red plaid jacket and a ludicrous straw hat, whose front brim is folded flat; "BILL" is inscribed there in red paint. Two ragged pheasant feathers jut from a hatband, denoting hunting prowess. Hartmann's olive jacket has "SMITH" in stencil letters above his left breast pocket. They both notice I don't have a shotgun, but say nothing.

I step atop a gleaming rail and gingerly keep their pace, my shoes making a tap-dancer sound. We hike down the straight tracks, grateful that railroads always take the shortest, most private routes. I've never seen more than two crows in the same place at one time and believe Bill's story to be false. We turn and cross a field, their heavy boots clearing a path for me through chest-high thistles.

We march toward a stand of hemlock when Bill signals a halt. From an opening beyond us, I hear a confused hum of shufflings and scattered caws. Perched amid saplings and clusters of lobe-leafed bushes, crows occupy the centre of a U-shaped clearing. Bill and me are going to circle, leaving Hartmann stationed at the opening to block any escape attempts. To the northwest, the woods thicken, and, when we reach our position, the crows are between us and a barrier of trees.

Bill hands me a yellow box of shells and we begin. Each squawk, each shriek intensifies, and it's plain we've been detected. It's so noisy I'm forced to cover an ear.

A sea of bobbing heads covers the ground like a rippling stadium tarpaulin. Branches bend in smooth arcs to accommodate squawking occupants. The crows compete for tiny red berries; they rape the bushes and peck each other in rages of greed. One bird leaps from his branch, frantically beats his wings, and flutters to the ground. These birds aren't drunk as Bill reported; most are too bloated to fly. Smaller crows retreat to the woods beyond, but the majority continue their indulgence in spite of our presence.

Bill inserts two shells into his double-barrelled shotgun and closes it with a snap. Signalling Hartmann, he drops to one knee, cocks the hammer, and aims into a crowded sapling. I've been instructed to pass two shells into his palm and stand clear when spent casings are rejected. One hundred metres away, Hartmann slams the breech of his gun closed and raises its barrel in readiness. It's clear we've entered a world not intended for humans.

Bill's first blast shatters the air; my eardrums ring in response. Again he cocks, sights, and squeezes the trigger. *Boom!* He breaks the gun, and two casings spiral to the ground; a stench of sulphur bites my nostrils. "Shells!" he yells. I slap two cylinders into his opened palm, like an intern assisting at surgery. An unexpected blast from Hartmann's direction makes me flinch. Bill smiles.

Fluttering and squawking, the crows are in chaos. Their numbers work against them; wings become entangled, foiling attempts to fly. Where Bill has fired into loaded branches, twin holes poke through the blackness. Leaning forward, he aims at the base of a crowded bush. *Boom!* His body jerks up with the recoil of the gun. In its panic, one crow hovers above us. It flaps its wings to escape, but Bill blows it into an inkblot of swirling feathers. "Shells!" Bill shouts, waving away down-fluff. I barely hear him through the liquid hum in my ears.

Some of the crows fall to the ground, others scurry through the grass toward Hartmann. Some flap their wings, crane their necks, and scold, but remain imprisoned in their branches. Hartmann concentrates his blasts on those who manage flight, his left arm pumping with mechanical precision. Bill can hit three crows with one barrage. It's evident from his cursing that he considers it a miss if only one falls. Hartmann lowers his weapon at the black army advancing toward him. His first explosion pours through their ranks like a splash of soapy water on a ship-deck, lifting and transporting those in its wake.

Drops of rain hiss against Bill's hot gun barrel, but he continues his shooting oblivious of weather conditions. "Shells!" he yells, blowing at smoke billowing from the breech.

A thunderclap booms across the terrain. The OPP must be on their way. "It's starting to rain!" I shout, relieved at the possibility of leaving.

"Good," Bill says. "It'll muffle our shots." I hear the clink of shell casings dropping into a pile at my feet. "Come on, we've got to chase them toward Hartmann!" We advance, Bill firing once every three strides. It's like walking through a ploughed field, clods of black bodies occasionally squishing under our feet, the sensation plastic and awkward.

A crow deliriously wanders about the ground, dragging a broken wing. I stoop, hypnotized by its misery. It trips and falls forward on its side, desperately clawing at the earth for traction. I reach to help, but it pops its smooth head between twisted wing feathers into a contorted position of defence. Eyes shrivelling with betrayal, it arches its neck to peck my hand. Instead, its eyelids squeeze shut, muscles relax, and it rolls over on its back. An eyelid pops open and an empty black sphere gazes at me. I scoop up cartridges from the shell box. I drop them into my pocket, and tear the cardboard into a sheet. Covering the crow's body, I marvel at its design, reminded that things intended for a simpler function can be separated so easily from it.

When we rendezvous with Hartmann, a squadron of crows approaches head-on as if in attack formation. They are flying at eye level, their silhouettes barely visible against the backdrop of trees. In his haste to reload, Bill grabs a jammed shell casing and burns his fingertips. "Damn it," he winces. "Quick, Jim, gimmie two more shells!" He loads, waits for Hartmann and takes him.

Their first volley flashes with the ferocity of a howitzer; two crows erased in the blink of an eye. Bill's second shot hits its target, too, but the bird's inertia carries it into his chest. Bill pushes it to the ground and squashes it with his boot. Hartmann's second burst is true, and the largest crow, bomber-sized in comparison to the others, dives to the ground. Watching the crows falling like black snowflakes, I'm amazed at Bill's and Hartmann's skill at killing. Two crows peel off in an escape manoeuvre, but Hartmann's capable pump gun sweeps them to obscurity.

"We got 'em, Hartmann! We got every one of them!" Bill pushes his hat back. "Did you see how beautiful that big one rolled off and dove to the ground? Just like a Snowbird."

"Guess what, Bill?" Hartmann inspects his remaining ammo. "I hit that big one with my deer slug. You remember that deer slug I showed you?"

Bill nods. He blows at blue smoke rising from his barrels. "Hey, Jim." He slides a shell into the left chamber. "I want you to hit that crow in the tree over there." He closes the gun with a snap of authority and offers it to me.

I had hoped that Bill, consumed in his frenzy, would forget about my participation. Yet, like a substitute player sitting on the bench, I've been rehearsing all afternoon. "I'm not a very good shot," I say, not really wanting to be heard.

"Take it," Bill thrusts the weapon into my hands. "And don't miss."

I plant my feet, pull back the hammer, and raise the barrel. Raindrops poke at the shoulders of my jacket; one ricochets off the stock and splashes into my eye. I squeeze my eyelid, accept the brief sting, and shake my head. Bill sighs impatiently. Raising the front sight into the crotch of the v, I fix it on the silhouette beyond. My target twists its neck in puppet fashion against the pink colouring of the uncertain sky. I hunch my shoulder, tighten my grip, close my eyes, and pull the trigger. *Boom!*

"You missed!" Bill grabs the gun, breaks it open, blows at the chamber, and inserts one shell. "You don't sight a shotgun, stupid. You aim it with both eyes open. And don't pull the trigger, squeeze it." Bill hands me the gun. "Don't miss this time – this is the last one."

I wipe my brow, seat the gun butt against my shoulder, and pull the hammer back. I take a deep breath, raise the barrels, and sight according to Bill's advice. Suddenly, the crow kicks away, flaps its wings, and climbs toward the horizon. I follow it and calculate its path. Hatred in the dying crow's eye nags my mind, but it's erased by my passion for success. Squeezing the trigger, I can almost see the pellet pattern sink into the feathers. "I got him," I say, exhaling. Wings spread like sagging semaphores, the crow glides down breast first, bouncing in slow motion as it hits the ground. I feel a surge of triumph. I try to push my face into a smile.

Bill slaps my shoulders. "Nice shooting," he says, taking the gun.

Sheets of rain force us into the woods seeking shelter, but sunbeams isolate the clouds and begin melting them. Each imprisoned with our own thoughts, we view black specks dotting the landscape. Blotches of blood coating tree branches, bushes, and grass begin washing away. Divots in the ground smooth their sores. Severed branches remain, permanent scars to today's memory.

When sunlight finally blasts through, we cross the open peninsula toward the tracks, the ground sucking at our feet. Bill ransacks the largest black feathers and adds them to his hatband, his singed fingertips provoking an occasional grimace. In a show of humanity, Hartmann plods across the field, finishing off dying survivors with his gun butt. I pick up a shell casing and blow on its open end, the lonely whistle recalling the dead crow's eye and its echo of emptiness.

Beneath the bridge, I wash mud from my shoes with a gnarled twig. I notice a brown spatter of blood on my pant leg. It's partially dry, and I splash cold creek water on it to prevent a stain. Gusts of wind, already frigid, push at bushes along the bank sending messages of winter to those who are listening. I gaze at Bill and his Medusa-like headdress. A feeling of sardonic ridicule blossoms inside me, but humility pacifies the notion.

J. B. JOE

Cement Woman

I'm going to dress all in greys today. Grey socks under grey boots, grey pantyhose under my grey panties, grey bra under grey slip, grey sweater over a long, grey skirt . . . grey blouse.

This is my grey day.

There's just a silver of purple light squeezing through a critch in my purple blinds. The dawn has arrived. I lie on my narrow cot, holding the edge of my quilt just under my chin. My body is perfectly straight, my toes aligned. I can feel my body settle into nothingness. In the far corner of the room a spider is preparing a web. She's a big, black spider, with red-gold tinges underneath her belly. Could be she's pregnant. I narrow my eyelids to slits, my pupils get large and the web becomes blue and dust flies from it as she works. There are sparks flying every which way, slowly becoming more and more blue until the room is filled with blue dust. Blue sparks from a pregnant spider. Outside giant ravens clink-clink together as they swoop over the river. I blink and the room returns to its normal hue. My body is in stillness underneath the quilt. I hear the stream running quickly and rippling along the jagged edges of yellow grasses clinging to the shore. A raven lets out a long screech.

There is always time to fling away the everyday.

I would hold the ashtray just under Wustenaxsun's chin. He would tell me to fling away the everyday. He was too weak to hold up his head, and sometimes to blink. He would lay there on his deathbed, telling me over and over again. There is always time to fling away the everyday. Always time. Always. I would flick the ashes from his cigarette with a long-handled paintbrush (number seven) as he sighed into his sleep. He wouldn't take long drags, just little intakes of breath to smell the smoke. He lay on his bed for four weeks like that. People came, but only to the doorway. He would no allow anyone else in the room.

The spider continues to work slowly and precisely. I get up from the cot and pick up my drum. The drum holds a new song for today and I beat it slowly, slowly, taking turns about the room. The light from the blinds follows as I beat the drum. I beat faster. I place my knees wide apart and spread my legs. I can feel pulls from deep in my stomach. I take small steps, increasing the speed of the drumming. The song is about a woman who learns all the ways of the hunt. She studies stories about Raven and his trickster ways to hunt. She studies how the air changes when a big animal enters her territory. She studies how her own body slips into the very breezes until she smells like her prey. Pieces of flesh line her bag. Flesh of the deer, the bear, the bait. She kills and recovers life for the old and for the children. The veins in my arms stick out like blue ribbons on the back of a garter snake. I can feel the pull in my stomach becoming almost unbearable. I continue to drum and to move about the room, with the new knowledge that the pain I feel is a signal. I feel myself falling forward and I stumble, but do not miss a beat. I feel the importance building and building. The song turns to high notes that last and last, my head tilts further and further back, and I can feel my hair brushing the small of my back. The song tells of the woman hunter entering the body of the deer. She feels his fear; she feels her blood rushing from one end of her body to the other in flashes of hot, lightning-like rushes. I kneel further back until the back of my head touches the floor and my pelvis is arched upward. I stay that way, letting the drum fall.

The song is ended and I get up slowly and I see that I have left blood on the floor. I go over to my dresser and open the top drawer. Inside is my jar of *tumulth*. I spread the red cream on my face until I see only my brown eyes. I go to my full-length mirror and proceed to spread *tumulth* all over myself. There is a soft coolness all over my body as the cream mixes with my sweat.

I walk like that, through my kitchen and then through my small living room and out the door. Outside it is cool and the sun is shedding its first light. The light hits the tips of the trees and casts long, thin lines of white dust-lines between the trees and among the branches of cedar. I place my feet into the stream. The yellow grasses tickle my feet. I enter slowly and walk to the middle of the stream until I am submerged. I close my eyes and I can feel my pupils filling everything.

I open my eyes and I am in a cave filled with the old ones and a golden light surrounds them. They have red bodies and all are naked. Their hair flies about their faces in a beautiful slow motion as they dance around a fire. I can feel Wustenaxsun. He is near. Oh, dear, dear Wustenaxsun. My husband. I see him. He is coming to me. I know that smile. I enter his eyes and we laugh together. He is restored to youth and he is strong again.

The flames from the fire light the cave until it is as bright as daylight, only, with a golden glow. The old ones come to Wustenaxsun and me and they kiss the tips of our fingers. They float away and continue dancing. They begin to chant, "The Mother of All Things waits," over and over again. There is a new knowledge for me. The Mother is waiting for me. I feel that knowledge very strongly. It tells me that if I turn to the entrance of the cave, she will be there. I am filled with the desire to see her and I turn. She is not there. I turn back to the fire and I find myself walking into the flames. Wustenaxsun lets me go and I can see him walking away as the flames wrap themselves around me. The *tumulth* crumbles from my body. I hear the chanting become faster and then all I hear is the whu-whu-whu over and over again. The flames unwrap themselves and I step out of the fire.

From deep inside of me I feel steel glowing red-hot and hardening all in the same instant. There is a movement of time that hits me. It feels like slow motion and divides itself into FLASHES OF FRACTIONS OF SECONDS! I scream. My pupils grow inside my eyes, filling everything. The steel becomes hard and cold. I align my toes and make my body still. The steel helps me. I close my eyes.

When I open them, I am in a shopping mall. There are people hurrying by me and they are grim-faced. Some of them pull angry babies. I look down and I am pulling my own angry baby. I have all grey clothes on and I turn to a man with powerfully built arms and legs. I smile at him. He wears soft, rich woollen clothes and he picks me up by the waist. The child falls on his face and screams. I scream. Blood falls from my eyes and I push the man away. He disappears and I close my eyes.

I open them and I am on a large, white ship and I am ordering *Oncorhynchus kisutch* from a waiter. I use only my eyes to place the order. He scampers away yelling, "The lady wants coho!" I wear a gold dress. The dress has no top and my breasts rest on top of the table. There are eyes sitting on the edges of the table and I glare back at them. Blood begins to fall from their sockets and I drink it from cups placed at exactly measured intervals around the table, which turns from square, to oblong, to round as I pick up each cup. I find an eyeball in the cup, too late. It slips down my throat. I yell, "Take a number!" and it pops back out. I pick up a fork and poke at it. It winks at me and wobbles away. I reach down to pick it up and the gold from my dress falls from my body like dust and scatters underneath the table and then it changes into the entrails of a deer. I put my face into the entrails and enter a room of spinning lights.

I fly and weave in and out of shadows. There are pinpricks of lights in my eye and they annoy me. I look down and I see that I have wings. They flutter only at the tips. They carry me about not by my power, not my power. It is the power of this room. Tears drop from my eyes and my pupils grow into everything. The dancing lights fade and everything is white and then darker shapes form themselves. The shapes are the people in the cave and they have stopped their blood. Time does not move. The shadows are still against the white walls. I breathe and my breath comes out in streams of pink and blue and orange and turquoise and purple and red and green and yellow.

I know she is here. I feel her blinking at me. The blinks are slow and steady, like a heartbeat. I turn away from the shadows and see an entrance. I hear the whu-whu-whu and it becomes more and more insistent, yet not louder. She stands there. She is blinking slowly, slowly. Blue air surrounds her. She sighs and her breath, too, is pink and blue and orange and turquoise and purple and red and green and yellow. I see my colours blending with her breath. She sits down, cross-legged.

I fly over and land just to her right. She turns to me and I enter her eyes. "I am the Mother of All Things," she says with her blink. Lights from our breath dance around our bodies and twinkle in the pupils of her eyes.

I tremble and she blinks that we, she and I are mothers. We are mothers of gods. Indeed, she says, you are the mother of Wustenaxsun, who is himself a god. She said she was the fire and the water and the coloured air. She saw me before I was born. She told me I existed in the fire and the water and the air. I told her I was lonely all my life. I told her Wustenaxsun came and made me a whole new life. She said yes, he did that. She blinked that I, too, made my new life. She told me my new life was my own wish. It was the wish to become who I am. It was the wish of the cave-dancers. It was the wish of the Mother of All Things. It was my own wish. We are one. We are one with our wishes. She blinked these words at me and I sighed into her breath.

I blinked that I lived with the cement people. They wished me to be one of them and I lived as one of them. I lived a life in the cold streets. I performed before them, dancing in the dimness of a beaten-down old beer hall. I made them put dollars into my clothing. I closed my eyes. She said you do not live among the cement people, now. I opened my eyes and she blinked my life. She blinked that I live in the mountains. I live in the forest. I live in the house beside the stream. I live with the ravens. The steel bends inside and I am sad. She emits a long stream and her breath captures my breath. She closes her eyes and fades away. The coloured streams turn back to white.

I close my eyes, feeling the tears dropping onto my breasts. I open them and I am back in the cave. The fire is no longer burning and I see Wustenaxsun's image on the cave wall. I see images of the old ones on the cave wall, their hair flying in graceful folds in the hard rock of the cave. I fly back to the shopping mall, through the hurrying crowd of grim-faced people and back to the white ship and back to the stream. I walk out of the stream and go back into my house.

There is always time to fling away the everyday.

Wustenaxsun would sit in the chair and tell me over and over that our life together would not be ordinary. He told me he would see that I would not miss the cement people. I would assure him that I did not miss anything of the town, the long roads, the noise of the traffic. We would go to the stream and bathe while he sang the songs. He would sing and the ravens would clink-clink in the trees. He made our song about our meeting. It told of a dying man who wished to have a wife. It told of a young woman living in the land of cement. She was dancing for money in a run-down beer hall and he sang how he, Wustenaxsun, travelled into the land of cement and found her. The song told about how she struggled with her past life after she moved into his house. Wustenaxsun sang about how her past belonged with the crumbled rocks at the bottom of the ocean.

I go and take my grey clothes from my closet. They fit me perfectly and I pick up my rattle and, suddenly, I hear the Mother of All Things. She tells me to put aside fear. She tells me the steel remains and keeps me strong in the face of real substances. The substances that make up the cement, the fire and the water and the coloured air, are also the substances that make up my own self, the same substances that make up the Mother of All Things. She is in the cement. She is all. She is one. We are one.

I shake the rattle and I see my future. It contains my children. Their faces are smiling and round, their heads shining from their bathwater. They run and hide among the trees and count petals that fall from their fingertips. My children. I am a mother. I am a child.

I put away the rattle and the steel inside remains stronger than ever. I will go and find my future. I will go and find my husband who waits in the land of the cement people. Wustenaxsun found me. I will find my husband. I already picture him in my mind. He has brown hair and brown skin, golden from the sun, and his eyes have pupils that never narrow down. Who knows but the wind and the rain that the man is not blond? I am at the centre of the universe. I place the rattle in a soft cloth bag.

DANIEL DAVID MOSES

King of the Raft

There was a raft in the river that year, put there, anchored with an anvil, just below a bend, by the one of the fathers who worked away in Buffalo, who could spend only every other weekend, if that, at home. The one of the mothers whose husband worked the land and came in from the fields for every meal muttered as she set the table that that raft was the only way the father who worked in the city was able to pretend he cared about his sons. Her husband, also one of the fathers, who had once when young gone across the border to work and then, unhappy there, returned, could not answer, soaking the dust of soil from his hands.

Most of the sons used the raft that was there just that one summer in the usually slow-moving water during the long evenings after supper, after the days of the fieldwork of haying and then combining were done. A few of them, the ones whose fathers and mothers practised Christianity, also used it in the afternoons on sunny Sundays after the sitting through church and family luncheons. And the one of the sons who had only a father who came and went following the work – that son appeared whenever his rare duties or lonely freedom became too much for him.

The sons would come to the raft in Indian file along a footpath the half-mile from the road and change their overalls or jeans for swimsuits among the goldenrod and milkweed on the bank, quickly, to preserve modesty and their blood from the mosquitoes, the only females around. Then one of the sons would run down the clay slope and stumble in with splashing and a cry of shock or joy for the water's current temperature. The other sons would follow, and, by the time they all climbed out onto the raft out in the stream, through laughter would become boys again.

The boys used that raft in the murky green water to catch the sun or their breaths on or to dive from where they tried to touch the mud bottom. One of the younger ones also used to stand looking across the current to the other side, trying to see through that field of corn there, the last bit of land that belonged to the reserve. Beyond it the highway ran, a border patrolled by a few cars flashing chrome in the sun or headlights through the evening blue like messages from the city. Every one of the boys used the raft several times that summer to get across the river and back, the accomplishment proof of their new masculinity. And once the younger one, who spent time looking at that other land, crossed and climbed up the bank there and explored the shadows between the rows of corn, the leaves like dry tongues along his naked arms as he came to the field's far edge where the asphalt of that highway stood empty.

Toward the cool end of the evenings, any boy left out on the raft in the lapping black water would be too far from shore to hear the conversations. They went on against a background noise of the fire the boys always built against the river's grey mist and mosquito lust, that they sometimes built for roasting corn, hot dogs, marshmallows. The conversations went on along with or over games of chess. Years later, one of the older boys, watching his own son play the game with a friend in silence, wondered if perhaps that was why their conversations that year of the raft about cars, guitars, and girls – especially each other's sisters – about school and beer, always ended up in stalemate or check. Most of the boys ended up winning only their own solitariness from the conversations by the river. But the one who had only a father never even learned the rules of play.

One sunny Sunday after church, late in the summer, the one who had only a father already sat on the raft in the river as the rest of the boys undressed. He smiled at the boy who had gone across through the corn, who made it into the water first. Then he stood up and the raft made waves as gentle as those in his blue-black hair

– I'm the king of the raft, he yelled, challenging the boy who had seen the highway to win that wet, wooden square. And a battle was joined, and the day was wet and fair, until the king of the raft, to show his strength to the rest of the boys still on shore, took a hank of the highway boy's straight hair in hand and held the highway boy underwater till the highway boy saw blue fire and almost drowned. The story went around among the mothers and the fathers, and soon that son who had only a father found himself unwelcome. Other stories came around, rumours about his getting into fights or failing grades or how his father's latest girlfriend had dyed her Indian hair blonde. And the boy who almost had drowned found he both feared the king of the raft and missed the waves in his blue-black hair.

One muggy evening when pale thunderheads growled in from the west, the boy who had almost drowned, who had the farthest to go to get home, left the raft and the rest by the river early. On the dark road he met the king, who had something to say. They hid together with a case of beer in a cool culvert under the road. The king of the raft was going away with his father to live in Buffalo in the United States and thought the boy who had almost drowned could use what was left of this beer the king's father would never miss. The boy who had almost drowned sipped from his bottle of sour beer and heard the rain beginning to hiss at the end of the culvert. He crawled and looked out in time to see the blue fire of lightning hit a tree. In the flash he saw again the waves in the king's blue-black hair, the grin that offered another beer. The boy who had almost drowned felt he was going down again, and, muttering some excuse, ran out into the rain. The king yelled after him that old insult boys use about your mother wanting you home.

The boy who had almost drowned found he could cross through the rain, anchored by his old running shoes to the ground, though the water came down like another river, cold and clear and wide as the horizon. He made it home and stood on the porch, waiting for the other side of the storm, hearing hail hitting the roof and water through the eaves filling up the cistern. Later, out of the storm, he could still hear far-off a gurgling in the gully and a quiet roar as the distant river tore between its banks. The storm still growled somewhere beyond the eastern horizon.

The raft was gone the next evening when the boys came to the bank, and the current was still too cold and quick to swim in. No one crossed the river for the rest of the summer. The king of the raft never appeared again anywhere. In the fall, a rumour came around about his going to work in the city and in the winter another one claimed he had died. The boy who had crossed through the rain thought about going down even quicker in winter river water. Then a newspaper confirmed the death. In a traffic accident, the rain boy read. None of the boys had even met that impaired driver, that one of the fathers, surviving and charged without a licence. One of the mothers muttered as she set another mother's hair about people not able to care even about their kids. The rain boy let the king of the raft sink into the river, washing him away in his mind and decided he would someday cross over and follow the highway through that land and find the city.

JOVETTE MARCHESSAULT

Song One
The Riverside

Translated by Yvonne M. Klein

In those days, we lived beside the river. We were my grandmother, my mother, my father, and my grandmother's second husband. We lived as a tribe, in a great congregation of nerve cells and blood cells. And we lived with eyes in the backs of our heads to catch sight of the prophets of calamity with their volcanic eruptions of rumour. Black clouds, grey novenas, and violet scapulars. This tribe of Catholics, head over heels in the holy-water font! Bad news spurting everywhere, distributed free by the waves, by everyone, by the newspapers. From time to time one of my uncles or aunts or this or that cousin dropped by the neighbourhood. They stopped in for a chat which lasted a month. There they sat all day long, their two feet planted on the oven shelf, warming their hooves and talking about other people's misfortunes. In the days I am talking about, all I had to do was put my car up against their heads to hear the murmuring of the little hope-eroding worms inside.

Our house was built out of wood from demolished buildings and covered in grey tar-paper. Inside there were shelves made from Tousignant butter boxes and cardboard partitions. In spring and summer, the house was surrounded by fields of oats and clover, and by Mr. Beauchamp's cows, the Pépin sisters' orchard, our chicken coop, our dog Nip, our calico cat, and frogs, toads, and garter snakes. Crows and wild ducks were in the sky and, from July onward, hummingbirds, which came to drink with infinite delicacy at my grandmother's hollyhocks. A few tribes were scattered toward the north and west. Further up was the peony-filled

Protestant cemetery and the woods belonging to the Chapel of the Atonement where everyone collected on Sunday for High Mass. In this house, my first dwelling place on the Earth, there was a piano, a gorgeous, harmonious beast, a bundle of the essences of more than fifty kinds of trees. This piano, which was won once upon a time by my grandfather, John, an Indian who killed himself by drowning in rotgut, was the focal point of our winter evenings. With the arrival of December, we entered upon an ice age. It was as if, between one minute and the next, the ice and snowbanks broke like waves above our heads. Even those cheerful words we might have exchanged between ourselves did not succeed in keeping us warm. Grandmother ran her fingers over the keyboard . . . a little rush . . . warming up her muscles before attacking the Fire Dance . . . a fetus's jig in the heated womb. A depressed melody, a perpetual shiver.

In those days we lived beside the river. An utterly beautiful river, with its depths turned in our direction. My grandmother said that the river was a baby bottle for the whales and their children, formula which went to their heads and made them sing and snort out loud. The whales lived further upriver, rather far from us, but on beautiful summer evenings, if one used one's ears and a little imagination . . . a murmur in the air . . . a great stirring of the depths . . . a monumental door swinging on its hinges . . . there was a whale approaching . . . tacking . . . waving at us before leaving for warmer or cooler water. This river was a feast for the eyes, the cars, and the heart. Living beside a river, particularly one in a northern land, quickly teaches you the habits of eternity. You have the feeling that someone has personally handed you a flawless diamond, a secret, a gift. It is only a feeling . . . it is certainly true that the past is horrible and that nothing good can be expected from the future. But living beside a river teaches you one thing at least – to withstand. For here the earthen banks withstand the most extreme winters, the spring floods, and everything that can happen to us in the form of wind, snow, and torrential rain. In the river, the stones withstand the currents, the enormous forces of the water. The river itself withstands our poisons, our sewers, our oil barrels, our atomic waltzes, and the thousand bits of kitchen garbage you can smell a mile away.

There was no alarm clock, no nightmare-shaker in our house. The rooster woke us up at dawn. What a cock! As alert as a watch-dog and as sturdy . . . active and enthusiastic from beginning to end. You should have seen his crest! His barbs, his wattles, his spurs! Red! Red! Red as blood, as a glass of ancient liqueur. And his cry – enough to waken volcanoes and shake up sleepyheads. Our day began with his cry.

After the cock's crow, all we had left to do was have a pleasant day, and this is relatively simple when you are between one day and four years old and if all your reflexes are reflexes of love. When, moreover, you have first-grade antennae to detect sincerity in others. When you have an interior space which provides a haven and nourishment and you can bring your sincerity to the end of the world with you. The reflexes of hatred and rejection – those come later. When you are that age, you have known about the Moon, water, grass, and the eggs that come from the backside of a hen from the promised land for a longer time than you have known about film stars, professional athletes, or laxative ads.

And now that the rooster had crowed, our hens set about laying their daily sugared, coloured, decorated eggs, eggs whose function was also to assure the continuation of the species. An egg of love! A vital egg! World egg, Quebec hen's egg, laid beside the river. Luminous egg, laid by the celestial Goose from the land of Egypt. Aerial cgg, synthesized from earth and sky, laid by the great Plumed Serpent from the lands of South America. Swan's egg, laid in one of the holes in the night, from the lands of the constellations. Golden egg from the land of India, cosmic egg in the Hebraic tradition. Thunderbird's egg, hot as orange. The Egg of Creation, in Australia, Polynesia and Black Africa. Our hens laid one egg in the time it took us to say it, without making a big production out of it, in the time it took to speak to them and stroke their feathers, and the egg . . . everyone was around the table, appreciating the gift, the texture, the odour; no matter where you prodded it, it was always beautiful and good, nourishing, running to every degree Fahrenheit because it was full of the magnetic currents of our hens' dreams.

After breakfast, I would meet Maurice on the dirt road which crossed 60th Avenue. From there we would run down toward the river to look for a drowned body. We had found three since spring. Corpses inflated with gas and with whatever pollutes the air of an entire continent. Natural gas, made from practically nothing, a little water, air, death, clots of blood, rashness or wilful carelessness, and there you had before your eyes the most beautiful drowned corpse in all creation. Floating in the water, fouled among the reeds, and their eyes – with all the coldness of the ocean deeps, without the slightest trace of affection or hatred or any other human sentiment. You could place a newspaper over their noses and they wouldn't react at all, merely stare at it with every appearance of intensity.

At this point along the river, on this particular morning, we were about to have a storm. Even the frogs were beating a retreat toward the shore. Maurice and I saw a man passing in a canoe. The rain started to pour down, the swirls and eddies swept the banks, and the mud from the bottom, with its leeches, fossils, buried treasures, gravedigger fish and other water matter, began to tiptoe to the surface. The man appeared indifferent to all the river signs. We called to him, "Mister, it's dangerous!" He turned his head and looked scornfully at us. He was not at an age when one begins to listen to the voices of children. He whistled a little tune to underline his indifference to our warnings. We ran along the riverbank for some time, repeating, "Mister, it's dangerous! Mister, it's dangerous!" He never faltered or wavered from his course, denying our existence in his mind. What or whom was he thinking about while he paddled through that black water? About a miraculous fish? What could have ruled him so that he could deny the danger in that way? It became night over the river in the middle of the day. We stopped, out of breath. He went on whistling. His red shirt, his canoe . . .

At the end of the day, his overturned canoe came down the river, swinging from side to side. It was his turn four days later. The reeds at the end of the 60th Avenue dock decided to keep him. There was general pandemonium after we discovered him. Grandmother, who made a religion of the dead, first recited the prayer for the dying before telephoning from the gas station a mile from our house. You should have seen the cops coming in their wailing cars. Streams of them, at top speed, in clouds of dust! A half-dozen of these Colossi, ready to gut the drowned man and gag him if he even looked like hollering or making a move. Their swollen, congested faces, their bodies taking shelter behind their uniforms. These cops were red-hot. They had to beat somebody up and the drowned man wasn't budging. My dog Nip, who instinctively detested anything in uniform, was frothing at the mouth, barking, rolling his eyes, trying to bite the policeman in the calf. He just missed being kicked and beaten with a billy club. For a few moments, all the cops devoted their entire attention to Nip, the mad dog. It would have taken a neural electrician to disconnect Nip's furry synapse by synapse. Still and all! I took the dog into my arms and spoke some soothing words. What an ordeal for the poor little dog! His whole body was sighing and his back was wet with sweat.

They brought out their long poles with hooks on the ends. Then came the whole business of moving the body, of bringing him to shore. Jumping here . . . bouncing off there . . . touching the bottom . . . the water lapping . . . hard to untangle him from the reeds. Everyone was taken with a kind of fright, because they were all there – they had come from their houses, leaving their dinners with crumbs on their lips. The members of the Catholic tribes had come to see. And anyway, it was a nice day, not too cold. They stared at the appalling thing, the drowned man floating in the water, heading toward us as if powered by a mysterious engine. The drowned body was oozing, gassy, pallid; its skin was turning unearthly shades of blue and green. Maurice's mother, Belle-Béatrice, let out a scream and everyone drew back a step in perfect unison. The drowned man had just landed on the bank. At the last minute, his body was pulled out with the help of the poles. A large green tongue came out of his mouth. It could have been a thick blade of grass. After that, everything moved right along – some policemen disguised as nurses brought a stretcher, dragged the drowned man by his feet and covered him with a tarpaulin. Five seconds later, the cars drove off.

Everyone went home, their shoulders bowed, at the end of their endurance as if they had just been put to the torture. Belle-Béatrice took Maurice by the hand, spoke to him, and said something or other in a solemn voice, still deep in herself, acknowledging the death which she had just seen face to face. I said goodbye, see you later, to Belle-Béatrice and Maurice.

Goodbye, see you later . . . That meant pretty soon, when Belle-Béatrice lit the floor lamps in her living room, drew her curtains, took out a glass of whisky or caribou and drank it in one gulp, disturbed and agitated by something stirring which I could not name. Afterwards, she went to the piano to sing while her husband, a gloomy-looking man despite his red face, settled in his armchair to read his newspapers, a cigar screwed into the corner of his mouth.

Belle-Béatrice sat down at the piano and attacked, literally attacked, the first song of the evening. With great spirit, she sang everything. She sang in Italian, Russian, French, Yiddish, Spanish, American. She could prod and poke any song to an incandescent heat. For her, anything would serve to be embodied and enfolded in the abrupt splendour of each note higher than the last. If pressed, she could have sung in Polynesian or Chinese. What fascinated Maurice and me was not so much what she sang, but how she did it. The profound significance of her shrieks . . . Thirty years later, I still think that her shrieks could have lit the dark side of the Moon and raised the dead from their graves. We settled down nearby, at a slight angle, the better to see her extend the veins in her neck and vibrate her diaphragm. When she attacked her first song, Belle-Béatrice puffed out her chest like a very dignified, naturally insensitive colonel. But little by little, song by song, she relaxed.

She never sang that sort of music which dogged us everywhere we went – on the beach, to the top of the mountains. Even if she did sing something well known, she did not provide us with the reassuring pleasures of a universe of familiar vibrations. From one song to the next, from one shriek to another, Belle-Béatrice lost her restraint. Her feet pounded the pedals. She held nothing back! Beginning with tremolos, she went on to genuine sobs. They flowed from her body like a river of lava and glass. Belle-Béatrice mopped her wounds and went on more beautifully than before. She was no longer swallowing her rage . . . no longer throwing basins of dishwater on the fires of her fury. I think she was giving her body and her soul complete freedom. She was expressing something fundamental. And whatever she was expressing, she was discovering it at the same time we were. Apparently what she was expressing contradicted the parish priest's latest sermon on resignation and opposed what her life had been, her entire life, to this point. It was really very odd and it was extraordinarily stimulating. What she enduringly was, in the depths of her being, was based on the explosive foundation of her shrieks. That, in fact, was where she began. And she would go far! In the brief pauses which marked the end of each piece, we could understand her anger.

She really only got going after her sixth piece. No more rigid arms and shoulders. Her emotions appeared everywhere without restraint. Since the rush of her blood was no longer held back, her emotionalism could show itself. And with it came impulses, sensual delight, scraps of life in the lines of her hand, a mortal fever in her expression. The locks were opened and the motors revved. Old Lent's ashes were blown away! The windbag was deflated! Belle-Béatrice was throwing mud on it, spitting on it, farting on it! Her song rose to encounter her liberation. Her excessive joy made her look like a prophetess, a witch instantly illuminated by the light of a hundred stakes. Energy itself, primal energy, devastating, disturbing and incomparable, flickered before our eyes. A terribly alive, even frightening, energy. Belle-Béatrice came out of a thirty-year imprisonment to visit her son and me, and her husband, too, if he had only lifted his eyes from the newspaper.

And what about Belle-Béatrice's vocal cords? Those vocal cords? The membranous folds of the larynx had certainly been replaced by catgut, by the kind of fibre usually used for bowstrings. That's how she sang! That's how she howled! That's how she communicated, warning us against what lay in wait for us once we got too old to be altar boys. The message flow to stick like an arrow right in the bull's eye. And the arrow went on vibrating for a long, long time.

As she was singing, it seemed to me that her emotional facial expressions were linked to an urge to scream, to bite, to speak up – to say you make me sick, you oppress me, I'm just a burnt-out bulb as far as you're concerned, you have never looked me in the eye, you are scared to death, you wish I would put a lid on my agony. I am your little sacrificial host.

Belle-Béatrice's tongue was in spasm, even if the Catholic religion did not permit it, even if the clergy took a dim view of it. She was no longer swallowing her misery and rage. She spat it out! She threw it up! She spewed it all over the religious objects, the chasubles, and the other sacerdotal robes. I never saw that expression on her face during the day when she was washing dishes or taking out the garbage.

Maurice and I were in no way terrified or traumatized. We didn't want to call the police or the lunatic asylum. A rush of life! Peninsulas of hope! That's what we perceived in her singing. It was not a matter of calling for help; rather we felt a response in her singing, a response to our first pain, to our first feelings of distrust when confronted by the continent of scrap iron which was more and more taking shape around the borders of the country of our childhood. Although words could not have made us understand. Belle-Béatrice's shrieks communicated to us. We were neither blind, deaf, nor paralysed – we were receptive to her version of things and her aversion to them. All the muscles in Belle-Béatrice's thoracic cage were transformed into pure, uncontrollable emotion, emotion which especially could not be censored by a tightly clenched jaw or by the paralysis of what-will-the-neighbours-say. This was an emotion that could not be swallowed because it was primary, illuminating, and able to spread out in its absolute strength among the floor lamps and the cigar smoke of an uncomprehending husband.

She had to do it. She had to say it. Belle-Béatrice spat out her rage and bit into her resignation – calves, jugular vein, ovaries, womb, she bit into all of them, everywhere. She had stuffed down her resignation until she wanted to puke. She spat out her fury through every pore of her skin. She sang, she shrieked, she pushed forward and expelled out of herself every cry of rage she had not uttered when bringing children into this world, when subjecting her family, day after day, to the authority of the entire tribe, when submitting to everything all of the time. She sang so that she would not give up. She sang so that she would not die too young. She sang so that she would not have to bury hope.

"More! More!" we said, and leapt up to open all the living-room windows and the front and back doors so that everyone could hear. So that everyone could listen, even the ones in Bone Valley. Shrieks like these had to sweep across the earth and sky by every possible means, taking the roads, the rivers, the railroad tracks, and the wrinkles of sadness in the faces of those who had given up. Shrieks like these had to be made known so that everyone might fly off the handle and drop their pretences. So that every man and woman slumped in resignation might answer the call and take up the battle-axe and smash through impenetrable walls.

Belle-Béatrice stopped singing just before eleven o'clock to have a little shot of caribou and mop her face and underarms. Moulten armpits! Then it was that we could hear someone playing the piano – playing music very much like Belle-Béatrice's. It was coming from the other side of 60th Avenue, crossing two ditches, a fine stand of aspens, and a couple of apple trees. It was Grandmother answering Belle-Béatrice on the keyboard of her piano. And that made Belle-Béatrice laugh. And that made her cry. She huddled on the floor and listened and listened to the tune my grandmother was playing, sighing all the while and emitting little cries of pleasure.

Grandmother neither sang nor shrieked but what she was expressing in her music did not leave Belle-Béatrice unmoved. It was a different tolling of the bell, that was all. It was a kind of personal biography which took everything into account – the weather, the thickness or density of the blood at that particular moment, the state of the tear ducts, internal or external combustion, the irritation of the uterine walls, the condition of the globules which floated with the current of the eternal transformation of the corporeal machine. She didn't just put her fingers any old place on the keyboard. She used only one finger, which she placed on a precisely chosen spot. Then, under the vibratory effect of this finger, thousands of other keyboards surged from the piano. Through hearing the same old song and the same one-dimensional logic, this music had been forgotten for a long time. No, the tune she played for Belle-Béatrice, for us, for all those men and women who wanted so to hear that air was a music at one with the Earth, with its underground springs, its caverns, its earthworms, its thunder lizards, with germination, that vegetal and mineral epiphany ripening in the womb of a volcano or the palm of an ice floe. Grandmother's music was full to the brim. And Belle-Béatrice did not feel either surpassed or crushed. She stayed in the same position, a glass of caribou in her hand, for an incredibly long time.

It was already late, past midnight, and Grandmother raised her vibratory finger from the keyboard and turned out the lights in the chandelier, leaving only a night-light on outside so I could come home without scraping my knees. I kissed Belle-Béatrice and Maurice walked me as far as the first ditch, which was filled at that hour with phosphorescent-eyed frogs. The grass rolled up and unrolled itself in the bottom of the ditch, making little rubbing noises and tiny cries at ground level. All I had to do was cross the earth and gravel of 60th Avenue and then the lovely green stretch in front of our house and there I would be already in the shelter of the aspens. If I raised my head, I could see the armies of wings crossing the sky between Earth and the Moon, the Mother of the Grass. There were the bats, the angels of the dark who kept a vigil above us all night long. There they were, with their gentle wings!

Thanks to my grandmother, angels loomed very large in this period of my life. In her woman's head there was always the old mystical virus, the fatal and eternal triangle, the destiny of decay, the absolute Redemption on the condition that . . . It seemed clear to Grandmother that, because of my playing beside the deep river and my wild careening through the woods of the Chapel of Atonement and the cemetery to the east, the gravest dangers were threatening me. Add to these the buses on Notre Dame Street, the railway tracks swarming with all kinds of maniacs snugly tucked in the empty freight cars, not to speak of Sherbrooke Street with its heavy refinery trucks.

This angel story came from the dawn of time, in versions modified and improved by millions of grandmothers. For my grandmother, the past, the beginning of the world, had occurred only yesterday, really only five minutes ago, and not in a period lost in the mists of time. In relation to the past, she was like a cow in a meadow – perpetually chewing the cud. For her, the creation of the world, the appearance of signs and beings on earth and in the sky, was not an event that was finished, but something which was eternally alive and near at hand. She used the chain of the past, with its wheels, dynamite sticks, and murderous bursts as a springboard to encourage her to pursue her course. She fertilized the past with her woman's hope.

Concerning the existence of angels, she said to me, "Cross my heart and hope to die." She was alive and the angels were all around. So I had a guardian angel, a protector who helped me weave my life. This angel was not off playing the *viola d'amore* beside the Milky Way as the super-Catholic zombies of the parish would have you believe. Nor was it time to blow the Last Trump. "Let them say what they want," my grandmother breathed in my ear. "Not everyone is lucky enough to live beside a river . . . " She hinted that the others would rather live in a stagnant swamp where they could proliferate like bacteria. Indeed, someone had suggested this angel as a model for me at my birth. Since then, the two of us had lived on the earth with other people's angels.

Through Grandmother, the Judaeo-Christian tradition made me a gift of an angel. It was almost as much a burden as a necklace of scorpions. It was both my celestial model and my chance to survive. A chance to run . . . just like Jonah in the belly of the mother whale, in the womb, in the electric uterus which decanted Jonah on a beach to remind him that the world is not just a fish's stomach and that one cannot spend one's life diving without coming to the surface from time to time. This angel was an image of myself. Once it had been given to me, it was no longer possible for me to get rid of it.

It seemed that Grandmother inflicted herself and me with guardian angels the way other people inflicted daily confession and mortification on themselves. Every punishment is valuable when you are obsessed with the idea of the Last Judgement and the great final book in which are inscribed all the accounts meticulously kept century after century by the accountant-in-chief and his subordinates. Fortunately, Grandmother did not hold forth very often in this vein. More often than not, she put the Absolute firmly in its place and sat on it, not being the kind of person who lives full time with the Absolute, as men so often do. Abstract concepts were too backbreaking for her! The Absolute is stiff as a poker and hard as a cannonball. It provides the perfect alibi for giving up without causing comment. On the contrary, if you give up while invoking the Absolute, you will be crowned with flowers and dragged in an allegorical chariot. Saint Absolute, justify us! This is the most popular patron saint in town. His shrines cover the earth. There's a real epidemic of them.

This angel story was in some ways her temptation in the desert. Struck down each time, Grandmother collapsed in the sand and there was no one to pick her up and lead her to the Temple heights. There was no one to honour her efforts and her courage. The Angels – to her, her Absolute – her struggle against emptiness. According to the Fathers of the Church (those macho Greek and Latin Fathers, pimps and company), the angels escape the eventual deterioration of the flesh which results from desire. Every day, in fair weather and in foul, they are engaged in a symposium with essences – a kind of summit meeting. What sex are angels? Evidently they are handsome young men with wavy hair, which is sometimes transformed into flaming locks or even a chariot of fire. They wear resplendent robes, which billow when confronted by God. "It is as if each phenomenon of beauty is the fringe of their garments." If they should chance to leave their summit meeting and appear to members of the Catholic tribe, they generally do it in human form, but in a transfigured and glorified human form indeed. The extreme simplicity of their bearing is also always striking. A mysterious aura radiates from their bodies, but – there is always a but – they are unable to procreate because they lack physical organs, or, if you prefer, a penis, testicles, and sperm, which is individually their own. And if they could, what would they transmit? An odour of sanctity! A pair of wings! Some of them, risking everything just before the Flood, fell in love with the daughters of men, as it says in the patriarchal Bible. They were demeaning themselves, since the greatest sin for an angel is to love a woman. This is the greatest offence against God the Father. So God turned these amorous angels out. He showed them the door of his mighty fortress.

There are all kinds of angels – sinewy ones who roll back the stone from tombs, cooks who bake angel bread, messengers who bring telegrams, truckers who transport war, enforcers, hired assassins with murderous arms, wrestlers. Not to speak of the innumerable ethnic angels who inspire nations and races. The prophet Daniel, who knew what was what, speaks somewhere of the Prince of Persia, a kind of very rich, oil-producing angel. The Apocalypse carries on in this way, too. These angels can make themselves heard and understood. They are multilingual and well educated. Indeed, Zachary and the Holy Virgin had the Angel Gabriel (in Hebrew: the virility of God) as an interlocutor and he talked to them in a human voice. According to Saint Luke, the angels always express themselves very well, with never a stammer, a stutter, or the least anxiety.

What is really terrible about the world of angels is that they have neither skin nor pulp. No flesh and bone incarnation for them, no cutaneous reactions, no broken wrists and ankles when they undertake a mission of salvation. They represent complete asepsis, triangular sterilization, and cosmic castration! They are wholly mutilated and resurrected in the digestive tract of the Glorious God. Their little volatile and ethereal aspect, their haloes, their pairs of wings are all an ideal subject for a vaudeville skit, but no one would dare laugh at these impotent beings in billowing robes. They are white! White, white, white with nary a grease spot, oil spot, growth, or belly button. And most of all, not a spot of blood. Particularly no telluric red, no psychic impulses of female red.

Extinguished! Denied! The great universal magnetic current is not for an angel's muzzle.

Sitting near the stove in winter or beside the river to listen to my grandmother tell her tales . . . a grandmother's words for her little granddaughter. When she talked about herself, she put aside her mystical reveries and her angels of the Absolute. That was the way it had to be, since Grandmother was made to live in a four-dimensional space, the fourth dimension being precisely that visceral need she had to speak to me about her desires, her hopes, her irrational self. She had the gift of being able wholly to involve herself in her words, to incarnate herself in flesh and blood in her subject matter. For example, when she told me about the whales, she became a whale, and nothing existed except the whale. She knew the whale through the movements in her guts, her heart, her kidneys, her breasts. Whale's milk? According to Grandmother, there was nothing more nourishing. Then followed a detailed description of its odour, thickness, temperature, colour, along with a comparison to goat's milk, cow's milk, and the milk from rubber trees. Her words were my food and drink. No matter what or whom she spoke about, her speech sparked an immediate pleasure throughout my entire body. Her stories were almost always about flesh and blood creatures, and it didn't matter if the flesh and blood were vegetable, mineral, or animal. What she knew and understood about each and every thing was a recognition which was life-giving, which injected vitality. Listening to her was for me to listen to the collective voice of every living thing. The little creative solo for each species could be heard, drawing its music, its words, from the antediluvian residue, from the mythological dust. Grandmother's speech was a speech undissociated from the elements of dream.

My grandmother was also bold and innocent enough not to be silenced by a news bulletin or a radio announcement. She knew instinctively that a news flash or an autopsy taught you nothing about the hopes and passions which ruled a creature's heart, and still less about the great ocean current which had borne it up through its entire life. Grandmother's words, the words of a woman, were born quite quietly under the soles of your feet and came up and grew with an irresistable force inside you in an utterly gentle way. With her words, my grandmother led me to the great widening of the river where suddenly there are no markers and where you do not need a telescope or a microscope. Even less do you need proliferating exaggerations and clarifications, when everything is already there in the delta of a woman's words. Oh, the beauty of these cellular, multidimensional words, this speech which calls up every forgotten and remembered emotion. These words come from all over – from on high as well as from below, from the wet, the thunder-stricken, the swollen, juicy and cloudy. These words cure just as well as thermal, saline springs, as the fountains of youth. These words are red and blue and shellfish green and the rosy pink of tentacles. There is not a shred of religious or political oppression or any other persecution lurking in the depths of these words. No Hydro dam or police barricade can indefinitely contain these lunary words, this world-water-spirit in motion. This is speech which knows that even if it banks and curves and climbs again and falls like a stone into indifference, it will still end by getting there.

It was their total sincerity that was terrifying about these words. They did not remain within the boundaries which separate the world of the mad from that of normal folk. They encompassed both worlds and it was absolutely certain that if these words were shaken by the tragic spectacle of the world's disintegration, of tortures and mutilations, they were not disintegrating along with it. These were the flowing female words which spew out and submerge the petrified wisdom of the dead.

Women's words which fill up the aqueducts of your ears and the blood channels of your body from head to toe during the nine months when every human being, without regard to race, sex, or social class, is aquatic within the tender surfaces of the womb.

Words of continuance! Sybil's words! Words which ever find their centre in a cavern, a grotto, an abyss, or a uterus flooded with the waters of tears. Sirens' words in the continuous flood of the waters of time. Sirens' words which move and dive into the matter of words, caressing it so that it gushes forth all those words which are encountered in a woman's speaking. A nymph's words which are the words of all the running waters, of every spring. Sea-spray words, words which ramble, wanting to burst out of the framework and leave the subject behind. Moon words and other words, fishwives' words which periodically, mistressfully, restore us. Quintessential words!

In winter, I lived in our house at Island End with my mother. In summer, I lived there with my grandmother. That was how they decided to share my survival. So, winter with my mother was the season for mending and knitting, for buckwheat pancakes, and for chickens whose throats were cut every Saturday. It was a time of logs in the stove, of comforting warmth and the end of the day when the gutsy winds made us all cling to our beds and chairs, when the whole world in winter revolved in a flurry of snowflakes and ice cubes. Up above, in the loft, the chickens pecked on, singing away as everything became more and more impossible. Our chickens twittered the most when things got the most impossible. They had imagination to spare! They had tons of hope and continuity! They were going to die the next day, maybe even that night, their two feet stuck to the ice if we didn't keep the heat up, or next Saturday, with the axe at their necks. So what! They dreamed! They imagined one more egg. They set about making it, perfecting it, and with it, the capacity to dream of a warmer, more welcoming world.

On sunny afternoons, Belle-Béatrice, Maurice, my mother, and I went skating on the river. We turned toward the countryside and toward the great icy surface of the river so we might learn what winter's fate was to be. Was the ice still thick along the river's edge? Were there bird tracks on the icy fold? Had the great strokes of frost weakened the elms? Spring was not far-off and its signposts became more and more evident every day. Skating on the river provided moments of perfect relaxation. At night, we had no choice but to turn in on ourselves, but during the day, taking a walk outside ourselves did us good. On weekends, Grandmother joined us. With her enormous courage and her burning need to share everything with me, she asked us to teach her how to skate. Her first lessons were now over – she fell just as often as we did and laughed just as loud! She improved her style from one weekend to the next. Friday nights, coming from work, looking ahead to Saturday, she sharpened her skates, her mouth watering, laughing expectantly. You should have seen her leap on the ice with both feet together, with a spring in her arms and legs. With a great thrust to her back she reached top speed skating toward the middle of the river. At that speed, she could have turned back a tidal wave and withstood any psychological whirlpool. What enthusiasm! Hairpin turns, on one leg, on one buttock. Dizzying pirouettes! Jumping like a frog when her skate caught a rough patch in the ice. Gliding through the air with the wind in her face. Snowploughing to a stop. She took Belle-Béatrice and my mother by their arms, hands, and scarves and they launched into a wild run. Too bad if some natural obstacle got in the way that they didn't have time to clear or avoid. They charged right into it.

One day, Maurice brought two barrels and suggested a jumping contest. I turned him down, knowing that my legs were not long enough to clear the two barrels he had rolled out on the ice. My mother, who was skating prudently that day near the shore, also refused to jump. That left Belle-Béatrice and my grandmother, Maurice being as little as I was. They drew lots. Grandmother was it. She skated around the barrels a few times, studying the angles, measuring them with her eye, sniffling at them. She pushed them a little to the right and moved them up a few feet so she could make the most of the slope for her approach. She had the wind and the sun at her back. There could have been no more advantageous conditions for a first jump. Belle-Béatrice and my mother approved – it was best to take no chances.

Grandmother shot off in a lightning departure, speeding up as she went. When she was no more than a few feet from the barrels, she tried to rise into the air – but it was already too late! She didn't have enough time to pull herself from the ice high enough to clear the barrels. Her skate buried itself in the wooden belly of the first barrel and then both barrels and Grandmother with them began to roll and crash down the slope with a hellish noise. We thought the ice could never support such a din, a weight like that. Now Grandmother was on top of the barrels, now underneath, testing the thickness of the ice with her nose. Finally one of the barrels rolled away and we could see Grandmother stretched out flat on her stomach. No one dared to move – she was dead at least. Maybe crippled for life? Entombed in an icy coffin? Maybe she had lost her memory, had forgotten where the North and South Poles lay, or where to find a dream? As we approached her, we saw that she was making faces and laughing at the same time. Maurice turned toward his mother. "It's your turn," he told her. Grandmother was already on her feet and dusting off her knees and face. As well as could be expected, she went to the shore where she sank into a snowbank, saying, "I waited too long to take off!" And she set about making plans for her next jump, prophesying success, but not denying that she could just as easily scrape her chin on the ground – never mind – theories have to be tested and not just in the lab or in discussion, but in the field. Then she began a passionate consideration of wind strength and the disposition of the barrels. We got home rather late after skating ourselves into total exhaustion. All night long I heard Grandmother groaning every time she moved an arm or leg.

In the winter, Grandmother worked in the furriers on Ontario Street in the east end or Saint Catherine in the west end. My mother worked in chocolate or garment factories from spring to the end of summer. Seasonal jobs – a new way of reading the map of the heavens. They both had so much to talk about when they got home from work – what they had seen, smelt, touched with hand or eye, felt with their fingertips. The men and the women they had met at a bend in the street, in the middle of the sidewalk, in the scramble to get on a streetcar or get off a bus. It was all there! The words, the intonations, the hesitations, the stammerings, the latest news from the North Shore, or Cacouna, or Rivière-du-Loup. The thickness of the ice across from Quebec, the whales at Tadoussac, the deaths, epidemics, births, baptisms, and all the phenomena of human activity behind which incalculable forces are concealed.

After that, they made things up, stirring the soup, straining it for the fourth time, and adding spices and herbs. They could each exaggerate equally well and draw hasty conclusions when the fancy took them. They often said things they didn't understand themselves. And so what? It wasn't all that important since they knew that some day these things would be clear and meaningful to them. Their language was filled to the brim with images and predictions. Theirs was a living language, full of significance, and it rolled and rolled in a sinuous tide or in a straight line, crossing landscapes and certainties.

Things were different with my father and my grandmother's second husband. They talked very little, engaged as they were in getting to the peak of their day, death in their hands. They worked in the munitions plant in Saint-Paul-l'Ermite, working on a world blown to bits, a world on fire; that's what they were concocting. All day long they made incendiary bombs or penetration bombs for protected targets. Or they made fragmentation bombs which are especially deadly to civilian populations and animals. The factory worked night and day making mayhem and cries of pain and agony, all in the name of peace. They never talked about what went on, but by observing their long faces, we could imagine some of it. Now and then, despite themselves, one or two words escaped from their mouths. There were shovel loads of accidents at the factory. Oh, yes, there was a shovel which was useful for picking up whatever was left of those who were clumsy or too tired to concentrate on what their hands were doing. Sometimes they also used a saw to prune the branch of a tree around which some guts or scraps of skin had wrapped themselves. When a shell explodes in your hands, you make one hell of a leap in the air and the thickness of a ceiling won't stop you. Death eats into you on the spot. "He didn't know what hit him; he woke up dead," they told us each time someone was blown to bits. I knew this little sentence by heart, they repeated it so often. It expressed their fear and the resignation into which people retreat while proclaiming themselves heroes or victims of circumstances. Grandmother clenched her fists and invariably answered, "When you wake up dead, that probably only means that you never felt alive." They shook their heads, entrenched behind the fear of unemployment, of utter destitution – it's a good thing the government gives us work. They never went any further, happy to revolve in their own words. But the discussion didn't end there! Grandmother brought her rage out of the cupboard. She talked about Hitler, that bogeyman, that puppet, as if she knew him personally. "I hold it against him," she would say, "against all those Germans – if they would only stop and think for one moment about human life . . ." There was something about this slaughter which particularly horrified her and made her raise her voice. The two men tried to calm her down but they only managed to drive her to a frenzy. Then she banged her fists on the table and got up to spit on the stove, restraining herself so that she didn't break everything in the kitchen. Grandmother had no desire to temporize or compromise with the war. That slaughter was her living nightmare and we felt that it was not for her a temporary or gratuitous thing. This nightmare had become a full-blown part of her life, one earned by the sweat of her brow, one which put her at death's door but also in life's orbit. "Explain it to me! I want to understand! Why is there this war? Why another war? It's a worm gnawing at our brains and guts. Why is there always a war?" She looked at her son and her husband, expecting an answer, waiting for a sign. They did not know why either and if they had known, they would have thought their opinions on the subject of no importance whatever. "That's what's so horrifying," Grandmother would add. "You also think the war makes no sense – there are thousands, millions of us who think the same way, but it goes on anyway, and this will not be the last one, either. It's appalling! It's worse than a disease!" After an outburst like this, she went to her room, banging the door behind her. "She's crazy," her husband would say. "She wants to change the world," my father would reply. My mother and I would stay where we were, without saying anything, pretending we were busy with something, but our hearts would not be in it. Fortunately, it gets dark early in the winter, so it would always be time to go to bed. Upstairs, in the loft over our heads, the hens were once again, perhaps, dreaming of spring.

Because spring always did come in the end! Spring came with its flood, tides, breakup, and ice scattered across the ground, a force which exceeded all recollection. Sidereal, palpable Spring! There was the first flight of black, black, black crows with morsels of summer in their beaks. The clock struck the hour for spring cleaning. We took everything outside – wool and flannel blankets, mattresses, pillows, rugs, tablecloths, trash can bottoms, old cadavers, everyone outside, cupboard rats and cellar rats, lice, cockroaches, remorse, and battle-axes. We opened the windows to sweep the dust outside, to renew the oxygen, to get the grime off the mirrors and the grey matter. We also washed the windowpanes and the skin between our toes. We scrubbed our ears and scoured our belly buttons. Easter was almost here! No more Lent, no more penitence, no more endless patience. In Montreal, Grandmother made her farewell rounds – to the bookstore, the sheet-music store, the corner restaurant. To everybody on the bus and the streetcar. She stopped at the liquor commission to celebrate and when she got off the bus at the corner of 60th Avenue, a little bit tipsy, she came down the slope trotting, sliding, and finally actually running. She abandoned her dignity and restraint. She took flight, saying she had too many things to do before she died. In the fields and ditches, green growing things had begun to show their heads. Grandmother took a sniff to the left, a sniff to the right, one at ground level, lifting up a clod of earth and touching the branches of a poplar or an apple tree. There was an impatience in her heart and a tingling in her arms and legs because she would soon be collecting plants, picking the fragilities of herbs, their fortunate perfections, the sensual shoots with their interior miracles.

In the heavens, the Mother of the Grass was creating her flora, weaving without haste all kinds of herbs. Calming, fortifying herbs for those who are impatient and anguished. Spicy, burning, magnetic herbs with red within for those who are lifeless and melancholy. Absorbing herbs for the absentminded and overtaxed. Yes, oh yes, oh yes! The Mother of the Grass was giving birth to her daughters of vegetation, her daughters venerated in the Spring sky which follows on the heels of the Christian Holy Week. She was giving birth to herbs which aid the birthing of complete babies or of fetuses. To affectional herbs, for every affection, respiratory, cardiac, and intestinal as well as the other kinds. To herbs for pain, pains all over, articular pain, pains of anger, pains of patience, pains in the pit of the stomach and in the heights of the heart. And to herbs for predicaments, for the bending of rules. To herbs for children, for chilblains, for convulsions, for seizures. To herbs all golden from the light which is organized within them. Even to melting herbs which help bloody flows and floods of words. To unbinding herbs for shrivelled muscles and paralysed tongues. To hot and scratchy herbs for mental dullness, and let's not leave out inflamed, laxative, purgative herbs to stimulate the asexual and the impotent. There were even herbs for night sweats and for the agonized sweats at the foot of the cross and the door of the tomb. Herbs to sustain those who are on the road to the slaughterhouse to meet their destiny face to face. Stupefying herbs! Tonic plants! Tragic, mythic, wild grasses, weeds to the ignorant. Herbs of knowledge, herbs for old wives, for poor women, herbs for the imperceptible changes of time, so solidly planted in the time that the herbs make flourish. Herbs which grow naturally in women's hopes.

In my grandmother's life, the months to come would be filled with herbs. But in addition, she expected to rock on the balcony, to play tennis with Belle-Béatrice, to fish in the river, invent new tunes for the piano, pick strawberries, raspberries, ground-cherries, and apples, play cards without cheating, and sleep under the stars, not so much under Jupiter as under Venus. She swore she would give the skin of her belly and her soul a good airing and that she would read me some nice stories. But meanwhile, in the meantime, my mother left us every morning newly to go to work among the chocolate, heat, cocoa, sugar, milk, and chemical flavourings. And meanwhile, 60th Avenue filled up with people and cars. Comings and goings, horns, hi, how are you, it was a long winter, the winter's always too long, does it look like the crows are back? The water is still high! The river is even more beautiful this year. A commotion which confused our every moment. Here came the members of the Catholic tribes, through every door of earth and heaven, along with their children who jumped back and forth across the ditches.

From autumn through till spring, there were only two occupied houses on 60th Avenue – Belle-Béatrice's and ours. The four others were cottages, houses for one season only. Beside the river, just before the drop which led into the whirlpool, the backwash, was the Cavalier's cottage. Just across from it, on the other side of the street, was the Lacroix's cottage. These two families were related. My auntie! My uncle! My cousins! In each one of their heads there was a docile, well-oiled mechanism which ticked over all by itself, operating in the present traditional tense, the social imperative mood, the deteriorating future tense. When Maurice and I crossed the space between their two houses, we always unconsciously stopped, a little frightened, with a sense of having entered a forbidden zone. Here, between the houses, the air was different. A little muffled noise, hardly perceptible, a gnawing sound which never stopped – it was a bit like in the mountains where it is never absolutely still because of the differences in elevation, the flow of air from one valley to the next, from one waterfall to another. Here there was a break in the atmospheric equilibrium. The air moved! The air was stirred up! These two families glided through the air, one above the other, mounting guard, keeping watch, giving strangers the evil eye. This was not a place where one should expose a vital organ. This gliding, this constant surveillance, was the origin of the continual hot and cold air currents around their houses. They were very good at taking advantage of air currents. Crossing this zone was no time for indecision. They never went very far, no further than their relatives, even on the nights when the weather was bad. If occasionally they lost sight of you because of a cloud or a spot of fog, at the slightest suspicious shadow, they instantly sank and found a new vantage point lower down. They all, particularly the men, had a kind of good-natured air in common which could initially inspire trust. But if you were to talk to them for long, you would discover that under this good-natured manner lay a confirmed malice which, as they were on guard against you, was hidden in order that you might like them. As a matter of fact, this good nature was nothing but an absence of passion or emotion, a kind of negative quality.

There were nine children in the Cavalier family – five girls and four boys. Four of the girls, who were the oldest of the family, were superb creatures. Tall, with beautiful hair, the bearing of a queen, as they say, with narrow hooves and the slightly arched back which puts the finish on the swaying of the hips and ass. They always drew back, their whole bodies recoiling, at the least sign of any disorder or inconsistency in the world around them. The Cavalier girls were four Amazons! When they invaded the tennis courts and began to slam away at the balls, it looked as though they were performing a private ritual. All the members of this family with the exception of the youngest daughter, who was only six years old, moved about like cars with their emergency brakes on. They had a peculiar kind of muscular rigidity in their necks and chests. They were holding themselves back. Even their glance, that fleeting expression which appears in the eye at the sight of something pleasant or disagreeable, even this expression was withdrawn as far as the Equator. Look at them! They were constantly controlling and regulating themselves. It was if they were afraid of something. Or somebody. They were not explorers. I am convinced that in their magisterial and decided way, they had reduced the urge to discover something new to rags and tatters. Maybe they were afraid of finding out that they were different from other people, from the other members of the Catholic tribes, from their uncle and aunt across the way, or from their cousins. This fear of difference, of the abnormal, was certainly in their minds, inherited from I don't know whom or when. Desire must surely once have laid its egg in them, in the men and women both, but they had drawn back their shoulders and tightened the muscles in their throats to stifle this egg and keep it from growing. Each time they walked down the street, they simply made us want to tickle them, to make the whole Cavalier family writhe and wriggle at the ends of our fingers. Then they would certainly say something extraordinary; then they would certainly express their rage and desire.

Just opposite them, across the street, was the other half of the tribe, the Lacroix family. Four sons and a daughter. The sons were all named after the evangelists – Luke, Matthew, John, and Mark. Though they were handsome, there was a peculiar tyrannical note to their words and gestures. Theirs was a less strained beauty than that of the Cavaliers. Actually they straddled the boundaries, inches away from a human expression, from a smile which could illuminate the whole face. They also had that eagerness, that desire for revenge, if you thoughtlessly beat them at swimming or running. Next came the Laframboises' house – they were unremarkable and laughed a lot about nothing in particular. Two sons and a daughter. The daughter was an articulate teenager who expressed herself passionately. Her brothers said she was a crybaby who wept at the drop of a hat, who cried whether the answer was yes or no. But from what I know about Catholic tribes, I think the answer was more often no than yes, and that's what made Madeleine cry so much. Evidently she was highly moral and had been talking about purity and innocence for some years. "Our sister is a little crazy," her brothers said. "But she gets good grades in the convent school. She's always in the top three." What the soul doctor said was, "Madeleine is an idealist. And we know that idealism often leads to vice. It is essential that this little soul learn to control and moderate herself." Madeleine had screamed out loud one January night. No one knew why. The body doctor said it was nerves, the pressure of exams. They talked about Madeleine a lot on 60th Avenue. Probably the problem was in the uterus. They talked about you, Madeleine. You seemed to have a feeling about the world and yourself which was disturbing to those who were ferociously involved in your education.

Last but not least was the Lemieux family. Two grown-ups, obese and ugly, their bellies swollen with chronic constipation – get out of the way, we're passing. They had two flawless, sensitive blonde children who were absolutely defenceless against ordinary daily occurrences. Monique and Lionel were the same age as Maurice and me. We felt that we were becoming more and more threatened with a loss of our playtime. Concerned and moral people wanted to grab hold of us and prevent us from touching each other, from looking each other straight in the eye, from seeing our pink bodies. When they spoke about our games, it was with enormous distrust. These were people who had forgotten how to play, but who knew how to kill time buying and selling insurance against everything – against life, death, fire, and pickpockets. They did not understand that our games were the genuine foundation of our lives and that their pious advice and their distrust would only weaken us if we paid attention to them. Maybe that's what they wanted.

There they all were, the people of 60th Avenue beside the river. "Don't throw sand! Don't touch frogs! Toads are dirty! Wipe your feet before you come in! Wash your hands before you eat! Don't touch! Don't talk! Bedtime! Don't touch the earth!"

We were going to try, we would try to pass through the holes in the mesh. That would be our last game before shearing time!

BASIL H. JOHNSTON

Summer Holidays in Spanish

We made the best and most of everything, good and bad, those of use who had to remain in Spanish, while others went home for vacation, made our summer happier and more carefree than it had any right to be.

The week before the end of the school term was like an anthill, with prefects and brothers supervising students in dusting, mopping, polishing, painting, repairing all the classrooms, toilets, refectories, corridors, chapels, and fence posts to make them fit for habitation come September. During the clean-up, the boys going home for the summer laughed constantly as they prattled about the meals that they were going to eat or what they were going to do. For the rest of us, who had nothing to look forward to, the last week was dismal.

As bad as the week might have been, it was as nothing compared to July first, when our fellow students left. We could only stare with mist in our eyes and resentment in our hearts as we watched parents from Sagamok, Cutler, Mississauga, Garden River, Birch Island, and Thessalon arrive and then leave with their sons. Then there was Dave Solomon whom we called David Plug, from his chewing tobacco habit. Poor as he was, he nevertheless walked down from the village of Spanish to come for his sons and daughters. We ached in bone and muscle to see all the "Plugs" – Orion, Leo, Joyce, Lillian, Doris, and Eleanor – skipping on the road to freedom and happiness. All day, old cars came and went, leaving the school just a little emptier.

Of the students going home for summer, the majority went by boat. At 9:00 A.M. on the day of departure, the boys from Wikwemikong, West Bay, Sheguindah, Sheshegwaning, and Sucker Creek on Manitoulin Island lined up in the yard in front of the main entrance to the recreation hall to be counted. They then marched in two columns down to the wharf, where they boarded the *Red Bug*. After them came the girls from St. Joseph's under heavy escort of three Daughters of St. Joseph. They, too, boarded the *Red Bug* on the side opposite the boys. *The Garnier*, under command of Father Hawkins, towed the *Red Bug* from Spanish to Gore Bay, a distance of twenty miles.

By the end of the day there may have been thirty-five of us left in the school, lingering in the silence and in the shadows of the empty yard, recreation hall, and dormitory: Ojibway from Cape Croker, Saugeen, Parry Island, Byng Inlet, Chapleu, Missinabi, Golden Lake, and Timagami, and Mohawks from St. Regis and Caughnawaga.

Next morning after breakfast, we made preparations for our own summer vacation on Aird Island, two miles from the mainland. We loaded straw, bedding, clothing, and laundry bags on the democrat for delivery to the *Garnier*; we stacked pots, pans, dishes, spoons, knives, ladles, tin cans, butcher knives; beans, peas, tea, oatmeal, bread; pails of lard, beets, onions, beef, pork; a tarpaulin, sails, oars, paddles, boards, tools, flashlights, and a medical kit into crates and bags. Lastly, we lined up to be counted before boarding the *Red Bug*.

It took the *Garnier*, cruising leisurely, no more than a half-hour to tow the *Red Bug* and three punts that slid from side to side over the wash and threatened to break from their tow-lines and make off by themselves.

Hardly had the *Red Bug* touched the bottom of the sandy bay at the camp than we all leaped off to race to the lean-to that was to be our shelter at night and during rain, in order to claim and to stake out a sleeping place near a friend on the straw. During this rush, Father Hawkins and the prefects, who were to be our guardians, cooks, and doctors, said nothing, but allowed us to enjoy our freedom.

"Dis is my place. I'm gonna sleep beside my frien' here. And don' you snore and don' you piss on my blanket."

Only after we had all staked out our sleeping places did the prefect blow his whistle to summon us to work.

For the next while, we were busy unloading the *Red Bug*, willingly and cheerfully.

"Where's do you wan' dis straw, Fauder?"

"Where you put dis here pot?"

"Where you wan' us to put dis sad ol' mush?"

"Hey, Fauder, where you gonna keep de candies?"

And Father Mayhew, whom we called Joe DiMaggio, grinned as he directed the porters to deliver "peas over there" and "blankets over there" and "you know where the tarp goes."

Where the *Red Bug* was unloaded and the punts pulled on shore and tethered, the *Garnier* steamed back to the mainland, leaving us to all the comforts and freedom that only the forests, winds, waters, and rocks can provide, confer, and allow.

But before we were allowed to leave camp, there was more work to do.

This lean-to, damaged during the past year by winds, snow, and porcupines, had to be repaired. With birch-bark, leaves, boards, and driftwood, thirty-five boys soon patched all the cracks and chinks, and stopped up every hole against wind and rain. Because we constructed our beds with the same ingenuity as loons, but with far less care, they resembled a series of nests without eggs, or mice's nests. In quick order, after getting our own quarters fit for habitation, we scrubbed the picnic tables, gathered wood, pitched the tent for Father, and erected the tarpaulin above the tables.

While we were busy getting the camp in order, Father was brewing a meal in an enormous pot. Just what he was doing we did not know nor, from the results, did it appear that he knew what he was doing either, but, according to his helpers, Father opened jars of cut green beans and sauerkraut, poured the contents into the pot, then spilled peas, beans, carrots, potatoes, onions, bones, and meat into the boiling cauldron. As we left camp, Father was paddling and puddling the sludge.

At last we were free. Free of rules, free to come and go as we pleased, free to eat or go without. We got to know and cherish freedom as only those who have been denied it can know and cherish it, as only seven, eight-, nine-, ten-, eleven-, and twelve-year-old boys can exercise it.

There were channels and bays and inlets for sailing and fishing, the islands of Villiers, Passage, Otter, Jackson, Brown, and Green a quarter of a mile opposite our campsite for visiting and discovering.

Some of the boys, notably Alvin Naskewe and his brother Lloyd, my former confederates at Cape Croker, did nothing else but ride the waves and fish. With each flat-bottomed punt, equipped with only one oar or paddle, navigation of any kind was almost impossible. Even with oars, it was hard to control these crafts, which, caught by the winds, slid or slithered sideways on top of the waves. Nevertheless, Alvin and Lloyd claimed one of the better punts for their own use, or, in our own vernacular, "just hogging it, dem guys."

Now, use of these punts was supposed to be decided on a "first come, first served" basis for all the boys, but, by gettting up before the others, Alvin and Lloyd were well within the rules. Because no one really envied them, no one objected. Besides, having learned the craft of sailing from their father, Enoch, they were skilled sailors and navigators, poling the punts along the shore, paddling to the islands, and even sailing with the use of their blankets or shirts whenever the winds were favourable.

During season, there were patches and patches of blueberries, which meant money. For each pail picked and delivered, we were credited with twenty-five cents, which was recorded in a little black book in the same manner as our ancestors were credited in trade for beaver pelts. At the end of the picking season, which lasted about three weeks, some of us had amassed a small fortune, accumulating as much as five dollars in our accounts.

Our only motive in picking blueberries was for money to relieve our hunger during the coming winter by bread-lard-candy trading.

There was a little candy store underneath the first-floor stairway, which was opened twice daily for fifteen-minute periods at twelve-thirty and again at six-thirty. With a small investment of two or three cents in jawbreakers, licorice twists, bubble gum, and suckers, one could drive a good bargain with his candy-loving but penniless colleagues, who congregated in the recreation hall just outside the doorway, waiting and pleading, "Gimme one, gimme one."

Except to friends, no one gave a candy away. The object was to tempt someone or several to make an offer. And luckily, there was always someone who preferred candy to bread or lard. The going rate then on the open market was seven jawbreakers for a slice of bread and five for a spoon of lard to be delivered either at the very next meal or at a time to be decided by the vendor of the candies. It was through this means that we got to eat an extra slice of bread on the odd occasion to allay our hunger.

Then there was hunting. For Charley Shoot, there was ONLY hunting. It was first and last. He was probably the only boy in camp, in the entire institution, who devoted all his time, from morning to night, to hunting rabbits, squirrels, partridges, groundhogs, beavers, skunks – whatever was worth hunting. I very much doubt that he ever went fishing or picking berries. For him, the day began at the beach picking pebbles, round ones that didn't curve. With a pocketful of ammunition, Charley would be gone for the day.

Charley preferred to hunt alone, rather than invite anyone too heavy-footed or too loose-tongued for the quietness that hunting demanded. Still, he asked me to go with him on a number of occasions, not that I was a good hunter or anything like that, but I was useful either as a decoy or as a porter, carrying extra ammunition or plucking the partridges that he killed. It was Charley's habit of walking directly through instead of going around swamps, hills, muskegs, ponds, thickets that provided us with excuses not to accompany him. Otherwise we might have gone more frequently and learned something.

Of the many hunting trips with Charley, I remember one clearly, and one only. On that morning and on that day, we were to hunt foxes, wolves, and bears, and I think he mentioned eagles and tigers. It was exciting . . . and frightening at the same time. Against whatever danger may have lurked behind rocks and stumps, I stuck right behind my partner, who, armed with a slingshot, frequently bent down to peer into the bushes or stopped to listen for some distant growl. For my part, I was busy checking which spruce or pine would offer the nearest shelter should bear or tiger come bursting out from ambush.

In front, Charley pushed on, his slingshot ready to fell bear or tiger. He stopped, held up a hand, and then knelt down on one knee. I, too, heard it. "Cluck, cluck" – the sound of the molars of bear or was it tiger? I looked around, behind, and to the front. Charley was drawing a bead upward, stretching the rubber bands of his slingshot well past his ear . . . steady . . . strong . . . dead on. On a pine limb sat an immense snowy owl, its hooded eyes half open in a kind of sultry way.

Charley fired. The eyes flew open, and the owl teetered on the limb for two moments before tumbling to the ground. He lurched to his feet, wings outspread, beak snapping, eyes rolling, unable to focus. Unsteady, as if drunk, the owl reeled from side to side.

"Got him jis where I wanted," Charley chortled. "We'll catch 'im an' take 'im back to camp . . . Gimme your belt."

I took my belt off without thinking and gave it to Charley.

"You stay in fron' o' dat owl; don't let 'im turn around. I'll sneak aroun' and catch 'im from behin' by de legs," Charley instructed me as he circled, crouching low. As if he knew Charley was up to something, that owl turned his neck, bearing his eyes upon my partner. Me, he ignored.

"Hey!" Charley stopped. He whispered loudly, "He's lookin' at me. Git 'im to turn aroun' and look at you. Do sometin'." Charley was angry.

With one hand, I held onto the waistband of my pants that were already sagging; with the other hand, I waved at the owl. I took two steps forward, calling at the same time, "Hoo! Hoo!"

The owl, perhaps perceiving the "Hoo! Hoo!" as a mating call, instantly turned. By now he had recovered most of his senses. When he saw me, he snapped his beak, then charged, half-flying, half-running. I went into reverse. With the owl gaining, I turned to sprint away. In so doing, I lost my grip on my pants, which fell to my ankles. I went sprawling. I covered my head.

In his rage, the owl pounced on my trousers, ripping at them with his claws and tearing at them with his beak, as if he were slashing at his favourite meal, the skunk.

At this moment of mortal danger, Charley hurled himself upon the owl and me. The next thing that I knew in my terror was Charley yelling, "Grab 'is neck, grab 'is head." I twisted around, got my hands on the owl's neck, and applied a choke-hold. By this time, Charley had wound my belt around the owl's legs and bound the owl's wings with his slingshot. I did not let go of that owl's neck until Charley told me to let him go.

Like big-game hunters who had bagged a trophy, we bore our prize back to camp in triumph. For all the indignity we had heaped upon him, knocking him down from his perch, wrestling with him all trussed up as a big white bundle through the forest, depositing him on a picnic table for all the boys to see, and then tying his one leg to the tree so that he wouldn't fly away, that owl stood on the picnic table with pride and looked upon us all as if he would take us all on. As if weary of the sight of us, he flew up to the limb of the maple tree directly above the picnic table.

After a couple of days, Charley untied the twine that bound the owl's leg. That owl remained in our camp for a week or more. During his stay, we fed him mice, birds, bread, fish, and scraps. But one morning the owl wasn't there. He was gone, summoned perhaps by his mate or by the spirit of the north. We twitted the perfect-in-charge, "Our owl woulda' stayed except for de mush you cook."

Even though the days at Aird Island were happier than those at the school, the loneliness was never far. The daily arrival of the *Iron Boat* with fresh supplies of bread, more green beans and "sad ol' peas," along with meat, also brought either happiness or sadness, depending on whether we received a letter or not . . . mostly loneliness and dejection.

But it was the occasional receipt of a letter from home that kindled hope and trust, and kept faith alive. At mail call, we'd congregate around the prefect who held a small packet of letters, opened and censored, in his hand. We'd wait for our names to be called.

Were we to get a letter from home, Eugene, Charley, Hector, and I would sit down together. The recipient would read it aloud to his colleagues. We didn't care about anyone's health or events at home; our sole interest in the letters that we received and the only message that we sought in the letters were the words, "You are coming home." And were they to be written, we could endure Spanish for another six months, a year even.

"Dear Brother," a letter to Eugene from his sister Delina read. "You're going to come home; you'll be home by Christmas. I've missed you, and Donald and Luke have missed you. When you come home we'll have loads of fun . . ."

Eugene just about danced for joy. "I'm going home for Christmas, I'm going to be home by Christmas; I'm getting out of here." Over and over, Eugene kept repeating the same words, and he laughed and slapped his thighs. We were glad for him, but envious, too. He was going home; we were not. Someone cared enough for him, but no one cared enough for us.

Eugene counted the days. He was even angelic in his mood and pious in his behaviour toward priests and teachers. Christmas came, but no one came for Eugene. That was the way it was.

Letters, almost every letter that arrived gave promise of going home. They gave us hope and they gave us faith to go on from season to season, from year to year. And, I suppose, they kept us in line, inspired us to obedience, lest we forfeit our chances for going home by misconduct.

Getting away from Spanish was never far from our minds. Feeling more neglected by his family after he had received a few cuffs from the prefect-in-charge for breaking an oar, Kitchi-Meeshi-Hec (Hector Lavalley) decided to run away from Spanish. Midst sobs and tears he took his leave of the camp, Aird Island, and Spanish by shaking hands with Charley and Eugene.

Instead of bidding Kitchi-Meeshi-Hec "goodbye," Charley and Eugene decided to accompany the escapee. They were not discouraged by their lack of knowledge of geography or the miles of blackfly, mosquito-infested bushes and swamps. Escape first; the details would follow. With Charley hunting along the way, there was little to worry about.

On the afternoon of the escape, Hector, Charley, and Eugene walked to the narrows at Little Detroit. At the banks of the narrows, the fugitives stood to regard the flow and pace of the current and the best manner of crossing the passage that was less than a stone's throw in width, but deep and swift. Even for strong swimmers, the crossing would have been dangerous. For Eugene, small and scarcely able to swim, it was almost impossible.

According to Eugene, Charley got that far-away look in his eyes, as if he could see something in the distance that others could not see, except that he was looking into the mass of rock on the opposite side. When the vision passed away, Charley spoke of his revelation.

They would pray for and work a miracle. Hector, almost sin-free would most likely receive the graces from Heaven to enable him to cross the narrows like St. Christopher. In the first crossing, Hector would bear Eugene; then Hector was to return for Charley.

For a while, they prayed mightily, but perhaps not with the degree of faith required for the enactment of miracles. Who of the three entertained the gravest doubt and thus aborted the miracle will never be known. It may have been Hector, who, too astounded by his nomination to imitate St. Christopher, failed to pray with the proper sanctity; it may have been Eugene for envying Hector; it may have been Charley for his inability to turn his mind from such worldly and material things as rabbits and moose long enough to dwell upon the spiritual.

At the end of devotions, which they conducted kneeling down and with great fervour right at the water's edge, Hector dropped to one knee to allow Eugene to get on his back. Even though Eugene was small and light, Hector's knees almost buckled, and he wobbled as he stepped gingerly into the water. Once he stepped into the water, set his foot on the slippery slime of the rock, there was no turning back. Hector slithered, Eugene struggled to dismount; both sank, hugging one another, and started to drift in the current out toward Shoepack Bay. Just a little way from where they fell in,

Hector and Eugene ran around and scrambled ashore, feeling like wet kittens and quite a bit less pious.

They returned to camp, having abandoned plans for escape. They would tough it out. I think that that summer was the last vacation Charley, Eugene, and Hector spent on Aird Island. Thereafter, as older boys, they remained at the school helping Brothers Van der Moore and Grubb with milking and feeding livestock and getting the hay in.

There may not have been much on Aird Island, but we wrought, from what little there was and what little we had, something bigger and finer and stronger. No one could see it, but it was there; no one could express it, but it was there. It was in each of us. With every new attempt or renewed attempt to achieve, our resourcefulness grew, and, as our resourcefulness enlarged, so did our spirit of independence and passion for personal freedom. We may have been deprived, but poor in spirit we never were.

At the end of summer, maybe a day or so before the students from Manitoulin came back, we left Aird Island and everything on it and everything that it represented – home, comfort, freedom, a place of growth – to return to exile, loneliness, confinement, and a feeling of repression within the walls of St. Peter Claver.

About the Authors

About the Authors

REDIVO PHOTOGRAPHY LTD.

JEANETTE C. ARMSTRONG was born on the Penticton Indian Reservation. She graduated with a Bachelor of Fine Arts from the University of Victoria. She has three published works: two children's books and a novel, *Slash*. Her poetry has been anthologized in Canadian journals. Her other creative work includes four produced video scripts, three music/poetry collaborations, and a storytelling mini-series, "Rattle-Bag," which was televised in the summer of 1989 by a local CBC affiliate. Her poetry collection, *Breath Tracks*, is scheduled for publication in the fall of 1990, and she is working on a non-fiction project in collaboration with architect Douglas Cardinal. Jeanette C. Armstrong lives in Penticton. She is the director of a multi-faceted Native education centre, which includes the En'owkin International School of Writing.

PETER BLUE CLOUD/ARONIAWENRATE is a member of the Mohawk Nation at Kahnawake, Quebec. He has been the editor of *The Alcatraz Newsletter* (1970), and a history of the Alcatraz occupation (1972). From 1982–84 he was the editor of

Akwesasne Notes. His latest book is *The Other Side of Nowhere; Contemporary Coyote Tales* (White Pine Press, Fredonia, New York).

JANE A. KRESOVICH

BETH BRANT is a Bay of Quinte Mohawk from Theyindenaga Mohawk Territory in Ontario. She was the editor of *A Gathering of Spirit: Writing and Art by North American Indian Women* (the first anthology of contemporary Native women's writing), and the author of *Mohawk Trail*. *Food and Spirits*, a collection of her short stories, will be published in the spring of 1991. Beth Brant is a mother and a grandmother and is currently living in Detroit, Michigan.

SHIRLEY BRUISED HEAD was born on the Peigan Reserve in Alberta in 1951. She is a member of the Blackfoot Nation, and has published poetry in *Fireweed* and *Whetstone*. She lives in Alberta.

JOAN CRATE was born in Yellowknife, Northwest Territories in 1953 but moved when her father, a miner, decided to go to university to become a teacher. She has lived in several places in British Columbia, Alberta, and Saskatchewan. Although she dropped out of high school, she attended the University of Calgary as an unmatriculated mature student, and earned an Honours B.A. degree in English, and a Masters degree in English, completing the first creative thesis allowed at that institution. Her work has been published in numerous literary journals. In 1988, she received the Banff Centre's Bliss Carman Award for poetry, and was runner-up in the Alberta New Fiction Competition in 1988. In 1989, she had two books published: a novel, *Breathing Water*, and *Pale as Real Ladies: Poems for Pauline Johnson*. Joan Crate is part Cree. She is married with three children and lives in Calgary.

RICHARD G. GREEN, a Turtle clan Mohawk, was born in 1940 in Ohsweken on the Six Nations Reserve. In 1973, he was an editor of the staff of *Indian Voice Magazine*, in Santa Clara, California, to which he contributed short stories. Other stories appear in anthologies published by Harcourt, Brace, Jovanovich, D.C. Heath and Company, and *Canadian Fiction Magazine*. In 1980, his cartoons began appearing in Native publications throughout North America. In 1987, he became a regular contributor to the "Our Town" column in the *Brantford Expositor*. His short stories, articles, and cartoons appear regularly in *Turtle Quarterly Magazine*. He lives on the Six Nations Reserve, where he is presently developing several writing projects.

TONY FONG

TOMSON HIGHWAY was born in 1951 on the Brochet Reserve in Manitoba. A Cree, he is the eleventh of twelve children in a family of trappers and fishermen. He studied music and English at the University of Western Ontario and in England, and is Artistic Director of Native Earth Performing Arts, the only professional Native theatre in Toronto, and one of only a handful of such theatres in North America. Tomson Highway has worked in all aspects of theatre including producing, directing, acting, and stage management, but is primarily a playwright dedicated to the development of literature of Native people. His drama, *Dry Lips Oughta Move to Kapuskasing*, winner of the 1988/89 Dora Mavor Moore Award for Best New Play, is the counterpoint to his equally successful play *The Rez Sisters*, a "delightfully earthy and achingly realistic character study of seven women on a Manitoulin Island reserve" (*Toronto Star*). In 1989, Tomson Highway won the prestigious 'Wang Festival Award.' He lives in Toronto.

J.B. JOE is a Nootka writer and a member of Penelakut Band. She has a B.A. degree from the University of Victoria, and has just received a Master of Fine Arts from the University of British Columbia. Her story, "Cement Woman," appeared originally in *Canadian Fiction Magazine*. Four of her poems appeared in *Whetstone*, and a radio play was a finalist in the CBC Literary Competition in 1987. J.B. Joe lives with her three children, one daughter-in-law, and one grandchild in Chemainus, B.C.

BASIL H. JOHNSTON (Ojibway) is the author of seven books, ranging from tribal literature and humorous stories to works on the Ojibway language. His titles include *Moose Meat and Wild Rice* (1978), *Ojibway Heritage* (1976), *Ojibway Ceremonies*

(1978), *Tales the Elders Told* (1981), and *Indian School Days* (1988). He works in the Department of Ethnology at the Royal Ontario Museum in Toronto.

JULIAN BLOCK

MAURICE KENNY, an internationally acclaimed Mohawk poet, was born near the shores of the St. Lawrence River. For many years he travelled and lived in Mexico, the Virgin Islands, and New York City. Presently he lives in the high peaks of the Adirondack Mountains where he is poet-in-residence at North Country Community College, having recently returned from the University of Oklahoma as Visiting Professor. Mr. Kenny has authored twenty books of poetry and fiction, his most current being, *Greyhounding This America: Poems and Dialogue*. His best-known collection is *Blackrobe: Isaac Jogues*; however, he was given the prestigious American Book Award for *The Mama Poems*. Widely published, his work appears in *Harper's Anthology of Native American 20th Century Poetry, An Ear to the Ground, New Voices From the Longhouse*, and *Earth Power Coming*, among many, many others. His work-in-progress, *Tekonwatonti: Poems of War*, is a collection of persona poems on the life of Molly Brant, the Mohawk wife of Sir William Johnson of the French and Indian War fame, who died in Kingston, Ontario in 1795.

FRANCISCO PHOTOGRAPHY

THOMAS KING is a Native writer of Cherokee, Greek, and German descent. He is a member of the Native Studies Department at the University of Lethbridge and is currently teaching in the American Studies Department at the University of Minnesota. His short stories and poems have appeared in journals in Canada and the U.S. He has co-edited a volume of critical essays on the Native in literature and has edited an anthology of short fiction by Native writers in Canada. His first novel, *Medicine River*, appeared earlier this year. He is currently working on a second novel and a screenplay.

ROBERT BARZEL

JOVETTE MARCHESSAULT (Montagneise-Cree) is a novelist and a playwright. Marchessault's titles, translated into English, are: *Like a Child of the Earth, Mother of the Grass,* and *Lesbian Triptych*. The plays which have appeared in English translation are: *The Saga of Wet Hands* and *The Edge of Earth Is Too Near, Violette Leduc*. A painter and sculptor as well as a writer, Jovette Marchessault lives in the Eastern Townships of Quebec.

BARRY MILLIKEN was born in February 1944, on The Kettle Point Reserve on Lake Huron. His tribe and language are Chippewa/Ojibway. His short story, "In Memory of Nelson," was published in *Ontario Indian Magazine*. Barry Milliken currently makes his living as a freelance commercial artist, with a view to shifting into the field of fine art. He lives in Dutton, Ontario.

© 1989 CHRIS BUCK

DANIEL DAVID MOSES is a Delaware born in 1952 on the Six Nations land along the Grand River in southern Ontario. He has been president of the Association for Native Development in the performing and visual arts. He is the author of *Delicate Bodies* and *The White Line* (poetry) and *Coyote City* and *The Dreaming Beauty* (plays). His work has appeared in *Whetstone* and numerous other journals. He lives in Toronto.

ROBERT SEMENIUK

HARRY ROBINSON (Okanagan) was born in 1900 and died in early 1990, several months after his eighty-ninth birthday. He was a well-known and much-revered storyteller from the Similkameen Valley in British Columbia. His blending of traditional oral literature with contemporary written literature has created a unique and powerful voice. Wendy Wickwire transcribed his only published work, *Write It on Your Heart*.

RUBY SLIPPERJACK is an Ojibway of the Fort Hope Band of Ontario. A mother of three children, she and her husband make their home in Thunder Bay, Ontario. She graduated from Lakehead University with a Bachelor of Arts and a Bachelor of Education Degree. She is presently employed at Lakehead University. *Honour the Sun* was her first published work. She is currently working on a new novel. Besides writing, she is a talented artist. Ruby Slipperjack has retained many of the traditional skills which most young Native people have not even had the opportunity to learn. As her writing shows clearly, her sense of loss and regret at the passing of a traditional way of life comes from the spiritual depth of her being.

EMMA LEE WARRIOR (Peigan) is a poet and short story writer. Her work has been featured in *A Gathering of Spirit: Writing and Art by North American Indian Women*, edited by Beth Brant. Emma Lee Warrior currently lives in Washington State.

JORDAN WHEELER, of Cree, Assiniboine, Ojibway, Irish, English, Scottish, and French descent, is the epitome of the modern Métis. Born in 1964, he began his writing career at the age of seventeen. Since then he has been published in newspapers, magazines, periodicals, children's books, and anthologies. *Brothers in Arms*, his first foray into "mature" fiction, came out in the fall of 1989. He has also written plays with inner city youth and a film for CBC. Jordan Wheeler has freelanced in the film and video industries to support his writing habit. He likes to travel, tell stories, and share his closet musicianship. Currently living in Winnipeg, he "stands six foot four, has two kids, and a sixteen-year-old cat."